A DINNER OF HERBS

A DINNER OF HERBS

John Verney

Better is a dinner of herbs where love is,
than a stalled ox and hatred therewith.

                              Proverbs xv 17

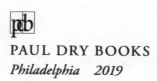

PAUL DRY BOOKS
Philadelphia   2019

First Paul Dry Books edition, 2019

Paul Dry Books, Inc.
Philadelphia, Pennsylvania
www.pauldrybooks.com

Frontispiece: John Verney in his studio, c. 1950

First published 1966 by Collins

Printed in the United States of America

ISBN 978-1-58988-132-7

To Sinibaldo Amatangelo,
Antonio Crugnale,
and their kind

AUTHOR'S NOTE

LIKE *GOING TO THE WARS*, this is a fragment of autobiography and belongs, since one is faced with the arbitrary choice, on the *non-fiction* shelves. It is in no sense a "sequel," but elaborates an experience briefly mentioned in the earlier book that, I felt, required a wider context and more allegorical treatment than could be given there. As before, the facts touching myself are true but I have taken liberties with most of the other characters, partly to simplify the story, partly to try to avoid hurting anyone's feelings.

An autobiographer is naturally reluctant to disclose where he has strayed from actuality in his efforts to present a more coherent truth. I would like, however, to record my debt to my old friends Martin Gibbs and Edward Imbert-Terry, most congenial of companions in adversity, and who, I hope, will forgive me for combining them, somewhat disguised, in a single individual. I wish also to thank Wilfred Thesiger for a tolerant understanding of my literary difficulties; John Grey Murray for permission to reprint the first chapter from the *Cornhill*; Clotilde Peploe for much help with research; Nancy Goodenough for innumerable hours spent on the typescript; Frank Del Signore for allowing me to use his name; and lastly my wife and children for listening so patiently and so often to an old tale.

A DINNER OF HERBS

CHAPTER I

In the early spring of 1943, the Beveridge Report arrived out in the Middle East, a morale-raising assurance that hostilities might end some day and that a benign Government was already taking steps to see that those who eventually reached home would find a less disgraceful state of affairs than they had left. I was camped at the time with a jolly band of pirates beside the ruined Crusader castle of Athlit, on the Palestine coast. The G.O.C. Middle East, or someone of that kind, personally forwarded the report to us, with a request that it should be carefully explained to all ranks.

We were legitimized pirates, about fifty strong and from most English walks of life, with the odd Greek, Pole, and Dane thrown in. The Upper Classes were represented by a Socialistic young peer, a truant Conservative M.P., and a morose Oxford don; the Lower by a poacher, a painter, and various butchers, bakers, and candle-stickmakers. But most of us were too young to have had much experience of pre-war employment—or, for that matter, unemployment. No one was over thirty-five, the majority were still in their early twenties. We were busy preparing ourselves for some, as yet unspecified, death or glory undertaking. Our days and nights were spent tramping energetically over thyme-scented Carmel, or landing canoes and dinghies on the rocks. Between whiles we tested our swimming powers across the mouth of Athlit bay or raced naked along the sands, watched inscrutably by our nearest neighbors, the few tattered Arabs who lived with their goats and chickens among the Crusader ruins.

Our parent body, Bomfrey's Boys, originally a small irregular
force founded by Matthew Prendergast and Oliver Bomfrey, had
paid the price of success and become a regiment, training in the
Canal Zone for some commando role. We were a self-contained off-
shoot, belonging to the Army but attached to the Navy and thus
enjoying the best of both worlds. That, and the incredible good fortune of finding ourselves camped on the Palestine coast in spring,
inspired us with an exhilarating sense of mission, a feeling of dedi-
cation to the task in hand, which came near to a sort of ecstasy—or
so it seems now, writing this twenty-odd years afterwards in middle-
aged decrepitude during another lovely spring. Certainly we were
all exceedingly healthy and exceedingly happy. So that the request
to stop splashing about among the rocks and surf, in order to study
a blue-print for Social Security in a hypothetical post-war Britain,
added merely a further touch of fantasy to an already delightfully
unreal existence.

Still, in fairness to Lord Beveridge, something had to be done
about his report. The Socialistic young peer, the truant M.P., and
the morose don all refused to be bothered, so the document was
handed to an Army clergyman who held a watching brief over our
spiritual welfare. He was asked to read it through and give us a talk
one wet afternoon. When the time came we modified our piratical appearance, assembled in the mess tent on the sands, and, with
appropriate solemnity, treated the occasion as something between a
Church Parade and a demolition lecture.

The padre had been to a lot of trouble and dutifully did his best
to put across the vision of Utopia, though he had to shout to be
heard above the hiss of wind in the dunes and the nearby lapping
of waves. "Every single man of you—I would like to repeat that—
every single man of you—whoever he is, will have to pay seven shillings and sixpence halfpenny a week to the Government. Of this,
the Government will eventually repay sixpence halfpenny a week as
an old age pension when you are sixty-five, or, if you are still earn-
ing, sixpence three-farthings a week when you are seventy . . . Now
about your wives. Every expectant mother will be entitled to receive
half a pint of milk hourly, I mean daily, and a third of a pint of
orange juice. That is *free*, or as near free as may be possible when
the time comes. Your wife will also receive a family allowance of five

shillings and threepence a week for every child after, and excluding, the first . . ."

"What happens if she only has one child?" asked the M.P.

The padre consulted his notes. "I don't think anything," he said, "but remember she will have had the orange juice. Now about the question of Unemployment Benefit, which I expect has been worrying you a good deal . . ." And so on.

All of us, except possibly the poacher, were in sympathy with the ideals behind the Beveridge Report. But how difficult it was to understand in detail! Besides, the wind had suddenly died and we were in a fever to get off and practice inflating a new consignment of rubber dinghies. I gave up attending after a while, to study the reactions of the others. In particular I watched a herculean sergeant, the hero of several raids on the Greek Islands. A few afternoons previously he had swum out in a rough sea to an M.T.B., drifting with engine trouble near rocks, and had towed it to safety. The exploit had caused him no trouble. But I can still vividly recall the glazed look of total incomprehension that descended on his cheerful features as his mind wrestled with the complexities of National Insurance in a world he was unlikely to see, and in fact did not see.

That evening, over dinner in the same tent, we inevitably discussed the report.

"Well, it's certainly a magnificent post-war target to aim at," said the peer, who happened also to be our Commanding Officer.

"I think it sounded absolute hell," said the M.P.

"No, much duller than that. More like the Kingdom of Heaven," growled the don, who, on a small scale, looked like a supercilious camel.

To me, as to the rest, the Beveridge Report was too far removed from present realities and pleasures to have more than a vague academic interest. But it did start my thoughts wandering in a direction that, for the past three and a half years, I had not dared to let them take—the idea of still being alive in the post-war world. From that premise my mind cautiously approached further ideas. They were secret thoughts and if my fellow pirates indulged in similar ones they too kept them to themselves. At a stage in the war when the end could not possibly be foretold, to make even the most tentative plans was to tempt providence. But in the next weeks, basking on a

slab of Crusader masonry fallen in the sea, or resting among the cis-
tus scrub on the sunny heights of Carmel, I began occasionally to
daydream of an existence shared some day with a wife I had not seen
for over three years and a son I had never seen.

The great question was—what *kind* of existence? At the outbreak of war I had just started on a career as a painter and, if I could
possibly afford it, I hoped to take up where I had left off. But the
many financial and other problems that being some sort of a painter
involved could wait till the time came. I was less concerned with an
eventual means of livelihood than with a post-war way of life.

For one thing, there was a basic choice to be made between town
and country. My wife, consulted by letter, replied that she didn't
give a damn where we lived, if we could only be reunited. In fact, by
upbringing and temperament, we were both essentially Londoners,
with leanings towards Paris as an alternative. Certainly a large town
would offer more chances for a struggling painter to pick up a living on the side. Moreover I was not by vocation a landscape painter.
My bent, so far as I had one, appeared to be for street scenes with
figures. London itself, preferably in a fog, was the most stimulating
visual experience I knew. I was especially interested in architecture
and the little training I had ever received had been at the Architectural Association—until I realized that I lacked the talent, or perhaps the patience, to become an architect.

All the same, like many Londoners, I felt a deep and frustrated
longing for an English countryside I hardly knew, except as a week-
end guest. I longed especially to learn more, one day, of traditional
country crafts and skills although I had only the haziest notion what
such crafts and skills actually were.

That spring on the Palestine coast these vague desires and impulses began to draw nearer to the surface, and to express themselves
in various ways, one being an enthusiastic interest in a neighboring kibbutz where we bought wine and dairy produce. Once, over
the mess table, I voiced my admiration for the erstwhile professors,
doctors, and musicians who, from hard necessity, had set themselves to scrape an existence from the barren soil. I confessed that I
felt drawn to emulate their example. My more sophisticated friend
Kempster, the painter among us, called it my *nostalgie de la boue*.
He had already been a professional artist for years before the war,

could explain such mysteries as offset-lithography or the half-tone process, and was equally at home discussing Matisse and the long-barreled Luger.

Kempster was something of a mystery. He spoke French, German, and Italian with equal fluency and revealed little of his background, except that it was cosmopolitan. Recruited by Matthew Prendergast from a secret intelligence outfit in Cairo he continued to wear his cloak and dagger with too much gusto for some tastes, though personally I found him a delightful and highly intelligent companion. A varied military career had included a spell with the Foreign Legion, from whom he had adopted the *shech*, a long wide cotton scarf that could be used also as a blanket and a towel and that added a touch of Beau Geste to his Byronic appearance. Consulted obliquely about a career in art, for I kept quiet about my own ambitions in that line, he gave the opinion that the only possible places for a painter to start were Paris and London. I have always been easily swayed by the opinion of friends and Kempster's advice influenced me far towards deciding on a town life.

Nevertheless my *nostalgie de la boue* could not be subdued. Apart from anything else I wanted my son, and any other children, to be brought up with an elementary knowledge, which I lacked, of the commonest birds, flowers, trees, and insects, a knowledge so easily gained in childhood, so hard to pick up later. That spring I resolved to do something about my ignorance and bought in Haifa a simple illustrated book on wild flowers, another on birds. Thereafter I was often to be seen stooping suddenly on dune or hillside to identify what proved to be merely a buttercup. But I had no memory for such things and the next day, as likely as not, I would have to identify the same flower over again—to the amusement of Philip, another close friend and fellow pirate.

A greatly gifted young naturalist, Philip Pinckney—I would like to record his full name, for he was killed soon afterwards parachuting into North Italy—was the least military-minded person imaginable. He never could see, for example, what it mattered whether a soldier had troubled to shave or not. But he had somehow transformed himself into a commando officer of repute and had been posted out to train us in our role of small-boat raiders. In appearance he looked like a humorous young god, good-natured in any circumstances, and it made you feel lighter-hearted just to be in his company; even Mark Duffy, the morose don, visibly brightened when he was talking to Philip. In my private deliberations between town and country, he pulled me far towards the country. With my flower book in one hand, some bedraggled specimen in the other, I would often seek him out in the store tent where he spent much time patching up, improvising or experimenting with our equipment.

"I say, Philip, I think this must be a variety of wild cyclamen, don't you?"

"Let me just fix this bloody valve." Then he would look up, his blue eyes regarding me with amazement. "Are you serious? It's an ordinary anemone."

"Oh, lord, is it really?"

"What an extraordinary chap you are. How can anyone possibly not know an anemone? I mean, it's like not recognizing a red admiral or a pied wagtail."

"But I *can't* recognize a red admiral or a pied wagtail. I wish I could."

"Nonsense. I don't believe you're as ignorant as you make out."

"Oh, but I am, I am," I would reply sadly.

And twenty years of trying haven't improved my ignorance. The little wildflowers, mauve, yellow, white, that arc everywhere bursting through among the apple trees in my orchard are still to me just lovely little nameless flowers. Only yesterday I mistook a blackbird for a thrush, to the amusement in this case of a seven-year-old daughter.

Influenced by Philip, by the kibbutz, and by the pleasures of the open-air, I came round increasingly to the idea of a post-war life in the country. I did not delude myself that I, personally, would be very happy in a kibbutz, but I dreamed idly of my wife and I creating something on a comparable, if less arduous, model in England. I might try to combine painting with farming, even though I didn't know a rook from a crow, or wheat from barley. Besides I loved farm machinery second only to London fogs. Those traction engines, their gold-banded black funnels puffing graceful wreaths of smoke over the harvest; or those strange beautiful monsters, like prehistoric insects in shape and colored the brightest reds and blues . . . I had seen them in the fields one hot week-end just before the war and had tried to paint them. How wonderful to possess one's own set of monsters, to arrange and rearrange them in groups at will, to be able to shout through a megaphone, "Move the blue one with the teeth a little farther to the left, next to the scarlet one with grasshopper legs." Of course the *business* of farming would eat up a lot of precious daylight and that would be a bore, but I might be able to dispose easels and canvases at different points on the farm, so that I could record the agricultural scene in odd moments when not laboring in it. Such a solution to life would demand a great deal of vitality and of steady determination. But at twenty-nine I possessed almost unlimited vitality and at least some determination, if not of the steady kind.

I learnt several new things about myself, then, that memorable spring, as well as learning how to plant a limpet under water or shoot a German in the stomach. The quickened interest in nature and a theoretical sympathy for those who worked the land were, I dare say, not much more than a healthy reaction to the pleasant circumstances of picnicking by the sea in the midst of a world war. But one discovery was of another kind entirely, and twenty years have done less to modify it. I learnt that, on the whole, I liked my fellow men.

I had never been too sure of it before. From almost as far back as I could remember, I seemed to have been in a more or less continuous state of conflict with them. The battle raged within, a perpetual inner tension towards mankind in general, a survival of the fittest attitude, bred originally at school and intensified by three and a half years of the army in war. Like the young David Copperfield, though for a different reason, I carried around a placard on my back which read, "Take care—he bites." I still wear it sometimes, but less habitually, and today I have fewer teeth left to bite with.

In our pirate camp the usual tensions of army life, and of any organized communal life, were reduced to a minimum. We were there at all by our own fervent wish, and were free to leave any time we chose. No one tried to parade his authority—there was very little of that sort of authority to parade. Nor was there much place for the detestable concept of one-upmanship. There was no point in pretending, for example, that you could swim better than you did, when your capacity was daily tested and exposed, and when— the vital point—there was no advantage to be gained by that or any other similar pretense. We pretty soon came to know one another's physical and mental capacities, and with them our own. Strength and skill were respected, and a fair degree of both were essential, but everyone recognized that there were other qualities, such as a cool head, or a good temper, that might well prove more valuable. On our type of operation the man who could make you laugh was more worth having than the bore who could only shoot straight. My greatly lamented friend Julian Lezard had little to contribute of conventional military value. But his courage, his wit, and above all his humanity, made him an indispensable asset.

The passing of twenty years has doubtless lent enchantment to the memory of the pirate camp. Certainly, as I shall presently show, our happy family was not more immune to violent storms than any other. Still, for two glorious months and as spring changed to early summer, the tensions, the formalities, the constrictions that had always bedeviled my existence hitherto, in peace or war, relaxed and faded away. A new Self began to emerge, one who no longer felt need of a warning placard. Life in the camp itself was such fun, my fellow pirates so amusing and delightful. An atmosphere of Bohemian sociability reigned in our mess where high spirits and a conversational free-for-all usually made up for what the cooking lacked.

Most of the credit for this happy, indeed slap-happy, state of affairs was due to the Commanding Officer himself, the Socialistic peer—it would be unfair to reveal his name for he has long since changed his political allegiance. In the best piratical tradition, he held the appointment by right of being the most experienced officer at small-scale raiding, and probably the most daring. Physically he was about as tough as the herculean sergeant, intellectually he could more than hold his own with the don or the M.P., and his vitality exhausted even mine. His title, too, was an undeniable advantage in wresting concessions from military and naval senior officers. He had the further quality, so endearing in the young, so exasperating in the middle-aged, of living in a permanent state of personal disorder. The same inner whirlwind that had made him a Lieutenant-Colonel at twenty-four, littered the camp with his socks, shirts, ties, and handkerchiefs. His trousers, when they were at last found, never had buttons. As the M.P. once commented with asperity, "He's perfectly splendid, but I do think a commanding officer ought to brush his hair occasionally." Having borrowed a Sam Browne belt, he would set off to some grand party in Haifa in the same pair of sodden muddy sandshoes that he had worn all day in a canoe, or would come rushing into the sea with the rest of us of an early morning without removing the dancing pumps he had worn all night. For, like most dynamic personalities, he was an ardent burner of the candle at both ends. He was young, gallant, gay, and, in things that really mattered, extremely efficient, and we all loved him.

The truant M.P. kept both ends of the candle burning pretty brightly himself. Also a small-scale raider of renown, he had joined us fresh from a daring high-level mission to—the Akond of Swat, I think it was. He remained an aloof figure, a planet that had somehow swum into our ken but which we must expect, in the nature of the universe, to swim out again before too long—who could tell where? Meanwhile he took a detached but friendly interest in our antics, like a tall and rather bald prefect who found himself temporarily mixed up in a troop of Boy Scouts.

But there were many other good friends, too many to name, and I think back with affection of them all. There was Edward, who had been through the desert campaigns with the Coldstream Guards; or Amos, my brother Yeomanry officer and close companion of earlier war days, now at the Staff College in Haifa. He called in frequently for a bathe and dinner and was hatching a private scheme to join us unofficially if we moved suddenly to a scene of operations. Oliver Bomfrey himself was too busy planning in Cairo to come, but Matthew Prendergast flew up from Egypt once or twice to see how we were getting on and to assure us we were not forgotten. Then there were more exotic birds of passage, perhaps using the camp as a base from which to embark on mysterious paramilitary missions—like Wilfred Thesiger, taking a parachute course on his way through from the Western to the Arabian Desert; or Walter Milner-Barry, the very picture of a jolly pirate, who had commandeered a caique in which he roamed the Eastern Mediterranean at will, occasionally provoking the whole Cyprus garrison into a state of emergency. But no one asked too inquisitively what the others were up to. Each of us was too happily, and, he hoped, usefully engaged on his own affairs.

Only the don remained morose. Mark Duffy was a military historian and, in a gush of after-dinner conviviality, I once confided that I had myself taken a history degree at Oxford. To my slight annoyance he did not seem surprised when I admitted that the result had only been a Third and thereafter treated me, more than before, as the sort of well-meaning barbarian to whom the war gave an outlet for energies that could find little scope in peace. Unlike the rest of us, he had never experienced regimental soldiering at first hand, so could not share our relief at being free from it now. A thin nervous man, he had grown an enormous R.A.F.-type moustache, which I suppose was his form of protective placard. Engaged on research work for the first three years, he had recently been commissioned into an Infantry Regiment, sent out to their Base Depot in Cairo, and from there, at his own wish, posted to us. By an extraordinary misunderstanding he had expected to find a well-ordered Officers' Mess, with batmen and silver plate and copies of the *Times Educational Supplement* awaiting his leisurely perusal over a glass of sherry. A certain amount of sand blowing down our necks, while we drank Palestine burgundy out of tin mugs and argued about everything under the sun, was part of the fun—after all, were we not pirates? But to the don such things were an ordeal scarcely to be endured. Our lack of normal military routine also struck him as quite abominable. He was romantic in his own way, and his vision of the army included much blancoed webbing, the stamping of boots on asphalt, and bugles sounding "on parade."

"What on earth made him ask to be posted to us?" Kempster said once, when Mark had gone fuming out of the mess because the tinned soup was cold.

"Just an excuse to get sent to Palestine, I imagine," I said uncharitably.

"I'm afraid the mistake was mine," said the peer. "I'd read his book on Napoleon, so when he wrote and asked if he could join I thought it would be amusing to have him. You can't tell how he may turn out on an operation. Yesterday I asked him to practice his men landing a dory on the castle rocks. When I went to see how they were getting on I found him sitting alone in the sun, reading the *Iliad* in Greek. I asked what had happened to the others. He said he had always understood that an officer's job was to lead his men into battle and that elementary training was best left to the N.C.O.s. He'd sent them off to practice where they wouldn't disturb him."

"What did you say?"

"Nothing much. I so envied him being able to read the *Iliad* in Greek."

"Oh, Mark's all right. In fact I think he's rather a good chap," said Philip. "I expect he finds us all a bit childish and you can hardly blame him. Really, he's just shy."

Shy the don may have been, but he was also—in true donnish fashion—sly. The trouble started with the latrines. We managed well enough with buckets. Our friends from the kibbutz came and emptied them in return for the valuable contents—so valuable that they even gave us a few bottles of wine and a cheese or two to clinch the bargain. From a distance, and against the evening sky, the buckets looked like the truncated columns of a ruined Greek temple, for the contractor who supplied them had failed to provide any kind of shelter or partition. Most of the pirates didn't mind. The site alone, with its view across the Mediterranean, was worth a visit. But the don's delicacy was outraged. He became more morose than ever and was to be seen stumping off every morning in the direction of the Crusader castle, the *Iliad* under his arm.

Then there was the business of the Palestine soup.

On the kind of small-scale raid we were training for, one of the hardest problems was food—how to carry enough to keep you going, possibly for weeks, both before attacking your objective and escaping afterwards. Pemmican, dates, biltong, dehydrated apricots, meat concentrates, and the rest, all provided nourishment for a time. You could live on them, if you had water. But, as Amos, Kempster, and I found to our cost later when we raided Sardinia, they didn't give enough bulk and you quickly lost strength. In a country with a friendly civil population, such as Greece or Crete, the problem might be less troublesome. But, even so, it was not hard to envisage circumstances where you had to hide on a deserted stretch of coast, taking care to be seen by no one. It would be silly to starve to death if all the while you might have been eating nutritious little grasses and weeds, had you only known what to look for.

The problem interested the botanist in Philip, it also appealed to my new-found enthusiasm for the soil, and we investigated it together. In fact we could claim to be pioneers, for at the time, so far as we could discover, there had been no scientific exploration in that field, though there has been plenty since. In any case, a system of trial and error was more likely to achieve practical results than any amount of theory. The peer gave our experiments his blessing. "You might revolutionize the whole basis of planning small-scale raids in the Middle East."

Philip and I confined our research to the immediate area of the camp, which should give the same range of choice as might be found, say, on the coast of southern Italy. We began to nibble at whatever we thought looked tasty. Nettles, dandelions, vetches, the stems of the juicier grasses, things like plantains, we dug them all up and ate them raw, or shredded and stewed them. "Here, try this, Philip, I think it's a mandrake root. Rather bitter, but not too bad . . ." But, as usual, I have forgotten the names of the plants. I can remember only their consequences.

When we ourselves had suffered no particular harm, and as our confidence increased, we felt that we should share our knowledge with the others—one day it might save their lives. The difficulty would be to persuade them to give the diet a fair trial. Like inducing a child to accept a new and doubtful medicine, we would have to use guile. We put forward a scheme to the peer who greeted it warmly. "An admirable idea. Just the sort of realistic touch our training lacks. We'll try it out first on the officers."

The idea was to make the officers really hungry by sending them off on an all-day march over Carmel, with nothing to eat but a packet of dates each. When they returned their dinner would consist, simply, of the plants that Philip and I had gathered. The peer was in favor of eating the plants raw, but we persuaded him that, at least on this first trial, it would be best to have them boiled into a soup.

Accordingly, a couple of nights later, an exhausted and irritable band of pirate officers, the peer himself among them, came staggering into the mess, exclaiming, "How I loathe dates," "What's for dinner?" "God, I'm ravenous!" "I could eat a haystack . . ." Philip and I had stayed behind to gather the necessary ingredients for the meal which was now served. The officers began to gobble it up until the don, after a few mouthfuls, put down his spoon and said, "What on earth is this revolting stuff?"

"Palestine Soup," I said.

"It's uneatable. What's the next course?"

"There is no next course," said the peer, and he explained that this was a surprise test of endurance.

"But what's the soup made of?" asked the M.P. suspiciously.

"Oh, just simple little things growing round the camp here," said the peer. "Things that you could easily find for yourself anywhere on the Mediterranean coast, if you were starving and had nothing else to eat. Personally I think Palestine Soup is jolly good," and he took a second helping.

"Just grasses and clovers and dandelions and that sort of thing," I said proudly. "Philip and I have tried them all on ourselves first, so there's no need to worry."

"Plus the odd snail, to help the flavor," said Philip. "Actually they could be eaten raw, but this time we've boiled them for you in sea water."

The M.P. quickly swallowed a glass of whisky before tucking in manfully. The others did likewise. But the don, after attempting another mouthful, said "Christ!" and hastily left the tent.

Later that night he was very ill. As a matter of fact, most of us were very ill. All through the hours of darkness ghostly figures flitted among the ruins of the Greek temple. The following day and night too . . .

Only the peer himself was unaffected. His many qualities included a cast-iron digestion. Soon afterwards he had to drive down to a party, or it may have been a conference, in Jerusalem. During his absence a certain listlessness was evident among the officers and several times I happened to notice the don chatting earnestly with the M.P. or one of the others in a corner. I thought nothing more of it, and when the peer on his return summoned a conference I imagined, from the unusual gravity of his expression, that we were at last about to be sent to our death or glory. Instead he announced, "I've got all the officers together because I'm told that there's a good deal of dissatisfaction with the way this unit is being run. We'd better have it out."

The peer glanced at the M.P. who, rather pinker in the face and less urbane than usual, rose to his feet. "Well, yes. There is. To my embarrassment, I've been asked to act as spokesman for various criticisms that have been made, but which I'm sure can easily be

smoothed out with a little effort from all concerned." No one, he
went on to say, disputed our commanding officer's gallantry in the
field, but we happened to be a military body and, to function effectively, a military body required other things besides gallantry from
its C.O. Its morale depended on a feeling of entire confidence in the
administration, on a reasonable degree of punctuality and order, on
a well regulated system, on a semblance at least of normal military
discipline. As a military body we were quite disgracefully slack. We
had no Adjutant, our webbing was never blancoed, there were no
morning parades, no drill, there was not even a bugler. For a start,
couldn't we at least fly a Union Jack on a flagpole, or even, in view
of our naval affiliations, a White Ensign? Really, at present, we were
hardly better than a rabble . . .

The M.P. was eloquent and plausible; he was not an M.P. for
nothing. Other officers murmured agreement. You couldn't beat
regular drill as a means of training. The men missed it, it gave them
a sense of unity. Perhaps we could improvise a parade ground on the
beach. Webbing was made to be blancoed . . . The don had been active behind the scenes. The peer began to lose his temper. "If anyone
thinks he could command this unit better, he's bloody welcome. I'd
be only too glad to resign and have some fun for a change, instead
of having to sit all day signing bumph . . ." The unmilitary-minded
among the officers rose instantly to his support. He was the perfect
C.O. for such a unit and the very idea of another was inconceivable.
Anyone who thought that we had time to waste for blancoing equipment or marching about on the sands obviously hadn't the smallest
notion of what small-scale raiding was all about and would do better
to go back to an Infantry Base Depot or somewhere . . .

The don spoke for the first time. He said boldly that he might
not have been a soldier for long but that he probably knew more
about the history of warfare than anyone else present. There was
nothing in the least new or original in our sort of small-scale raiding—he need only remind us of the Trojan Horse, or of Gideon.
What *was* original was our extraordinary attitude that we were, in
some obscure way, training ourselves better for this type of operation by poisoning ourselves with ridiculous food or wandering
about with fly-buttons undone. "The whole of civilization depends
on someone being prepared to give way," he said. He did not doubt

that our C.O. was splendid on an operation, but at present we were *not* on an operation and, until we were, he suggested that we accept the peer's offer to resign, and, instead, invite the M.P. to take over command.

There was uproar. In a matter of minutes all our happiness, our really exceptional happiness, had been shattered. Instead, two rival gangs faced each other, their knives and cutlasses drawn, and, with horror, I saw that in a second or two the gangs would close. In despair, I interposed myself between them in the very moment of collision, offering to take on the duties of Adjutant and to make myself responsible for the camp's administration and discipline.

The collision could not be averted, but at least the impact was deadened by my bruised and bleeding body. Knives and cutlasses were lowered, a compromise was reached, in the English way. Henceforth, it was agreed, the Jolly Roger and the White Ensign should fly together. Webbing need not be blancoed, but we would indent for a bugle, and someone to blow it. There would be no drill on the beach, but the contractor would be bullied into finishing off the latrines properly. And never never again would Palestine Soup be served in the officers' mess.

After that, everyone became friendlier and happier than they had ever been. The M.P. proposed a vote of complete confidence in the peer's fitness to command. The don apologized if he had appeared at all carping or critical but he had only been trying to do what he felt was his duty to the honor of the British Army. The peer said that he was proud to be in command of such a distinguished body of officers, that excessive training had made us stale, that there was nothing like a storm in a tea cup to clear the air, and that he himself proposed to have a bathe before spending the evening with Amos in Haifa, if anyone felt like joining him . . .

And the last of the lessons I learnt that spring in our pirate camp at Athlit was this—that if, like Abou Ben Adhem, you loved your fellow men, then you must expect to spend most of your life, not in painting, or in tilling the soil, or in trying to improve your knowledge of birds and flowers, or in any other pleasant and profitable fashion, but simply in trying to stop your fellow men from cutting one another's throats; and sometimes your throat.

CHAPTER II

WHEN I WAS LEAVING SCHOOL, the master who had been trying to teach me German gave me two excellent bits of advice. The first was to memorize a few quotations in a foreign language. "They'll come in handy," said the wise and genial man. "Even if there's never an opportunity to use them aptly, there will certainly be pauses in the conversation when a line or two of Italian, Portuguese, or Scotch dropped into the silence may help to break the ice."

Since then I have journeyed through life equipped with only two such quotations, both German and learnt from him. One is from Schiller.

Mit der Dummheit kämpfen Götter selbst vergebens.

"Against stupidity even the Gods struggle in vain."

The other is Goethe's epigram:

Alles auf der Welt lässt sich ertragen
Nur nicht eine Reihe von schönen Tagen.

"Everything in the world is supportable—
except a row of fine days."

Once, during the raid on Sardinia, I was able to quote the Schiller with some effect at a German sentry whom I needed to convince that I was an eccentric Italian officer wandering round an airfield at 3 A.M. The Goethe has remained, neglected but unforgotten, for over thirty years in the lumber room of my mind. Besides, in England, it seemed such nonsense. How could one ever have a surfeit of fine days?

Then last summer, near Florence, where I happened to be spending a few months with my wife and children, we had twenty-nine scorching cloudless days on end, and, though they were far from insupportable, I did at least see what Goethe had perhaps meant. I even began to hope secretly for a shower if only because the peasant on whose farm we were staying grumbled that the grape harvest would be ruined unless the weather broke. Watching him work all day in the fields in the heat, I was thankful for a septic foot that gave me an adequate excuse not to offer to help. I was thankful, too, to be in the comparative cool of a hilltop, rather than in Florence itself which in such weather becomes an airless oven. And I cursed a great deal when, on the twenty-eighth day, I had to put on a suit and tie and shoes, to go to a large formal lunch party, the invitation for which, in an unguarded moment, I'd accepted several weeks before. The first person I saw on entering the room was Matthew Prendergast.

Since the war we had usually met every year or two when he happened to be in England. Now, I learnt, he was in Florence for a few days on his way back from Persia where he had been mountaineering.

"Whatever are *you* doing here?" he asked. "Why aren't you on the Surrey kibbutz?"

For the first decade or so after the war I tried, in a lighthearted sort of way, to realize my dream of combining art with agriculture, at least to be as self-supporting as possible on half a dozen acres. I kept a cow, bees, poultry, pigs; sold the small surplus of fruit, flowers, and vegetables; and although I never—as Matthew and other visiting friends pretended to believe—actually wove my own clothes, I did make much of the pottery used in the house. The dream faded, the necessary vitality began to flag, and in any case I found I could earn more by a day's work on a drawing board than in a week of persuading local greengrocers to buy my admittedly not very successful tomatoes and lettuces. When the pigs had been killed I didn't bother to get more . . . But Matthew likes to keep his friends pigeon-holed and in his mind I am for ever a painter who insists on also playing at being a peasant on a small holding in the stockbroker belt.

"Who's milking the cow while you're away?"

"She died."

"The bees?"

"They caught Isle of Wight disease and had to be destroyed—thank God. You're years out of date. I've even given up hens. It costs a shilling to produce an egg, and you can buy one for sixpence—because of the subsidy. As I have also to pay for the subsidy my eggs were costing me one and six. Peasants have a poor time of it in England—and so much the worse for England in my opinion. We've let the house, said to hell with everything, and come abroad to draw a deep breath before deciding how to go on. I can do my work better here—fewer telephone calls. Among other things I'm trying to write a book."

"Where's Lucinda? Is she coming to this bloody lunch?"

"No, she's taken the children to the sea for a fortnight. I've stayed to work, but after years of family life I can only concentrate when I'm in hourly danger of being interrupted. So I'm off to the Abruzzi. Partly pleasure, partly to tie up a few loose ends of memory—I was there in the war. There's a little *festa* on the first Sunday of September at a place called Tollo near Pescara, which might be amusing. I want to see a P.O.W. camp and then climb a mountain and visit a cave near Sulmona. Why not join me? It's the wildest scenery in Italy and, as a connoisseur of the primitive, I think you'd enjoy meeting some peasant friends of mine—*real* peasants."

Matthew consulted his engagement book. "For how long?"

"Four or five days. We'd go by train to Rome on the Saturday and hire a *seicento*. Back in Rome by Tuesday night, Florence on Wednesday."

"Yes, that will do fine. I'd like to come. I have to be back for rather an important engagement on Wednesday afternoon."

The idea was thrown out on the spur of the moment but, as well as being glad of his company, it pleased me to take someone who, by launching me into Sardinia, had thus indirectly introduced me to the Abruzzi. Matthew was not likely to be much interested in my war-time experiences there—when any mention of his own far more varied and dramatic exploits bored him utterly. To him the war was an almost forgotten interlude that had delayed his true mission in life and that he'd shed from his system the minute it ended, to devote himself to the anthropological journeys with which his name is now chiefly associated. But it was precisely because of his hatred of twentieth century civilization and his passion for the untamed, wherever it could still be found, that I was so eager to show off the Abruzzi to him. The other guests were arriving and we quickly settled the arrangements before our host separated us.

"Bring your camera," I said. "There's some marvelous stuff in and round Sulmona."

"I never take photographs in Europe."

Apart from Matthew I knew no one else at the lunch, the atmosphere was stifling, my tidy shoes pinched, my suit and tie chafed, and I found myself seated between an empty chair, destined for a guest who wisely hadn't turned up, and an elderly German lady, of forbidding appearance and with a string of unpronounceable names and titles. From the awe with which she was treated, I gathered she was someone especially important, like a great-granddaughter of the last Austrian Grand Duke of Tuscany, or something. On the whole I was glad when she ignored me and talked exclusively to the neighbor on her other side, an elderly and forbidding Florentine gentleman who, I gathered, was also someone especially important, like the cousin by marriage of the great-grandson of Queen Victoria, or something.

The meal was wonderfully elaborate, but I lacked the appetite. However I enjoyed the different wines served with every course and a white-gloved footman kept refilling the array of glasses before me. When not emptying them again I strained to listen to Matthew farther along the table. He was talking with impressive fluency in French to a strikingly handsome and evidently amusing Italian Countess. More used than I to tropical life, he was more suitably attired, and his tall gaunt frame, like a splendid pinnacle knocked off the top of a Dolomite, was encased in a thin cotton suit already damp with sweat, as though the pinnacle had recently been rained on. From what I could overhear he was describing the curious initiatory rites of a Kikuyu tribe he had lived with. *"Les jeunes hommes, quand ils ont treize ou même douze ans . . ."* The Countess seemed fascinated, exclaiming *"Tiens!"* or *"Per Bacco! . . ."* at intervals.

As the weary meal drew towards its close, my own neighbor turned and graciously grappled with me in English, rightly guessing I would be inarticulate in any other language.

"I heard you are a painter?"

"Yes, a sort of painter."

"Do you paint portrait or landscape?"

"Well, actually . . ."

"I have a great friend who paints portraits. Perhaps you know him. He is called Pietro Annigoni."

"Well, I know the name . . ."

"And so you have come to beautiful Florence to paint?"

Of course she was not the slightest interested in why I had come to Florence, but I had drunk so many glasses of wine that, since she'd asked the question, I determined to answer it. "To paint was only one reason," I said. "Really I've come to try to recapture something. A zest for living, you could call it, or a taste for the essential things, for bread and cheese and garlic sausage, so to speak. It happens, quite often I believe, that a young man reads a book which influences the course of his life. Then he reads it again in middle age . . ."

"Ach, so you read a book as a young man?" She made the action sound vaguely discreditable, but excusable in a *young* man.

"I meant it figuratively. You see, as I grow older, and more tired, and more wrapped up in my profession, I begin to wonder whether I haven't made an enormous mistake by involving myself with a whole lot of interests and people that have nothing to do with my proper work and merely eat up time and money. I suppose I've come out here partly to relive an experience, to remind myself of the importance of disinterested human kindness, to relearn a lesson that I learnt in Italy during the war . . ."

It was a mistake to mention the war. Her grim old features clouded with an expression of hostile reserve that changed to greed as the waiter offered her a superb Neapolitan confection of ice-cream in various colors, dotted with nuts and layered with pastry soaked in rum. While she dolloped two or three spoonfuls on to her plate

I persisted doggedly with my confidence. "After living for eighteen years in Surrey, the lesson had begun to wear off. I felt it was time to refresh my mind about—well, about the good *basic* things . . ."

"Ach, the good basic things," she said, with relish. "And so you are finding them here in Florence, I expect?" She sounded a little skeptical, or perhaps bewildered.

"Well, actually, I'm living on a farm outside, with peasants."

"Ach yes, peasants. They are so charming," she murmured, tucking again into the *cassata*. "And how long are you here?"

"Since the early spring."

"And when do you return to England?"

"When I've watched them make their wine. About mid-October."

"And you are alone?"

"Well, my wife and children are with me but they've gone to the sea. To escape the heat."

That gave her the chance she needed to talk about herself. "Ach, how wise of them." It was as if I had released a spring and the conversation became an energetic monologue. As a rule, she said, nothing would induce her to stay in Florence for July and August, she *always* went to the sea or to the mountains. But this year, what with the expense of her new yacht, and the iniquitous taxation nowadays, and her losses at Monte Carlo, she had been forced to economize and stay on for a couple more months in her villa at Fiesole. "And now this heatwave!" she gasped, flapping a hand weakly to create a draught. "It would happen to me. I am *always* so unlucky!"

It seemed the golden opportunity to trot out my quotation from Goethe. And here I should mention my old language master's second bit of advice—which was for heaven's sake not to get your quotations mixed. Because, as I realized some seconds too late, I had quoted the Schiller.

"THE *IMPRESSIONISTS* IS RATHER a meaningless word, Leslie. It began as a term of abuse and then stuck. You see, some like Monet and Pissarro were chiefly interested in light and pure color. Whereas others, like Degas . . ."

Your bunk was your bed-sitting-room. It was cramped but comfortable enough, with straw-filled *pallione*, sheet, blanket, and pillow. The top berth had the advantage of a certain remoteness, it also had better air, and was in consequence usually grabbed by first-comers. I occupied, therefore, a bottom bunk, a shadowy recess from which I peered curiously at my companions. Leslie, my immediate neighbor overhead, was an exceedingly polite young man who had been a bank clerk for a short time when war started, but who dreamt of joining the Rhodesian police when it finished. He had mentioned, with apparent regret, that he knew nothing about pictures and I had embarked on a lecture, glad to share a pleasure and to disinter a few long-buried scraps of knowledge. But he soon cut me short, saying, "You must tell me more about them all sometime," and lay back on his bunk strumming a ukulele.

After the war kind friends occasionally asked if my experiences as a prisoner had been *Hell*. I could but reply, with a tolerable degree of truth, that on the contrary I had seldom enjoyed anything so much. For one thing, and for the first time in four long years, I was free to do entirely what I wanted, which was to read as much as possible and try to learn to draw and write. For another, an Italian

P.O.W. camp at that particular moment, August 1943, seemed to offer a pleasant temporary respite from the war itself.

Our band of pirates had dispersed earlier in the summer. The peer, the don, and the M.P. went off with half the force to raid the Greek islands. The rest of us, accompanied at the last minute by Amos, traveled via Egypt to Algiers to join Matthew and Oliver who had planned a raid to attack German airfields in Sardinia before the invasion of Sicily. The vicissitudes of the operation have been described elsewhere. Sufficient to say that, by the time a *carabinieri* escort handed us over at the gates of a *campo concentramento* in the Abruzzi, near the Adriatic coast, Amos, Kempster, I and the two other officers had had more than enough of adventure, enough too of ourselves. We were allotted bunks in different parts of the crowded barracks and, like boys from the same school arriving at a university, quickly lost sight of one another.

On first acquaintance, the camp really did have much in common with a university, one surrounded with barbed wire and armed guards, but where you had the chance to study, to make new friends, or simply to laze about doing nothing, as you pleased. You could take up pretty well anything, from chartered accountancy to aerodynamics, from bridge to baseball. There were language classes, lectures, plays, debating societies, concerts, an excellent library; or, if you preferred, there was the opportunity for incessant conversation. To which was added continual sunshine, sufficient *minestrone* and *pasta*, and a daily half-pint of *vino* that tasted like a mixture of red ink and vinegar but was better than no *vino* at all. And behind everything loomed the probability that the Allied armies would shortly invade the Italian mainland, to liberate us.

It all seemed a little too good to be true—and it was.

There were about fifteen hundred British and five hundred U.S. officers, under the command of a Senior British officer. The Americans had joined the camp recently, but most of the British had been prisoners at least a year, some for three years. A few were near the edge of despair, a few had passed over the edge, but the great majority had long since learnt to accept the succession of empty identical days with a patience that lay somewhere between philosophic resignation and plain lethargy. They were good, they were kind, they were civilized, and they were terribly bored.

Especially they were kind. Did I need pants, a sweater, a towel, soap? "Here you are, take mine. I've got plenty," said Leslie.

"But are you sure you can spare it?"

"Yes, really. I'm well off. Had a next-of-kin parcel last week. Besides, when you've been here for a while you collect masses of junk, as you'll find."

"Am much struck by the *kindness* of everyone" I noted in my diary. (Soldiers on active service may not keep a diary. Unlike so many generals I had stuck to the rules, thus denying myself this simple form of consolation, and now I plunged happily into one, my mind teeming with trivial observations that demanded expression.) But the little stir caused by a new arrival soon subsided and when my companions saw that I was fixed up they left me alone. "An atmosphere of live and let live" I jotted down. "What you choose to do with your time is strictly your business. But time lies heavily on most."

I was rather embarrassed at how little heavily it lay on *me*. By the end of a week I found I was enjoying myself so much that I almost hoped—no, I *did* hope—that the Allies would not liberate us until the Italian class had finished reading Dante's *Inferno* and before I had mastered a pen and wash technique that promised to be an advance on my pre-war efforts.

"You look awfully damned busy all the time. How do you manage it?" asked Polly with a touching note of envy. He had been a tea planter in Malaya, then a gunner in Tobruk, where most of the British were taken. He was gentle and shy, seldom spoke, and had given me a toothbrush. Guiltily, I put aside what, in fact, was the first draft of *Going to the Wars*. "Oh, not really. Just catching up on a letter to my wife." Making a pretense of yawning, I strolled off to sketch the camp.

The buildings surrounded a rectangular yard, large enough to take three baseball games at a time, with some overlapping of players. The cookhouse block and a hall used for theatricals closed one end, the main gates and Italian staff quarters the other. Three long dormitory-bungalows filled each side. Beyond the cookhouse, olive-covered hills reached up to the picturesque town of Vasco, its cluster of pantiled roofs crowned by the campanile of the duomo. To us, leading our austere monastic existence on the plain below, the view

offered a tantalizing glimpse of a happier reality. It was a daily tor-
ment to think of a civilian world thriving beneath the campanile,
to imagine streets with food and wine shops, with restaurants and
women, and children chasing one another over cobbles. A modern
glass and concrete hospital, that stood on the town's edge, added
emphasis to this idea of normal life continuing out of our grasp.

In the other direction, beyond the houses by the gates, the
ground lay flatter, revealing merely a glimpse of poplars and fields
that stretched miles and miles to the north-west, to where the mas-
sif of the Gran Sasso rose against the evening sky like a Dantesque
Mount Purgatory. At the end of August, the Camp Intelligence bul-
letin reported that Mussolini himself was now imprisoned on the
Gran Sasso. We seemed to be following him around, for he had pre-
ceded us by a few days in prison on the island of La Maddalena, in
Sardinia.

The yard had the character and charm of a piazza and provided
a subject almost ideally suited to the limitations of my talent, as I
now began to understand them afresh. My draughtsmanship, I recognized, lacked boldness. I could not compose a picture as Renoir,
Degas, or Lautrec had done, with a large figure cutting across the
picture plane. I preferred to see everything as on a stage, viewed
from the back of the stalls, with figures grouped and gesticulating
against a setting as nearly architectural as could be devised, and
with perhaps a glimpse of mountain or campanile between buildings. The yard, with its graceful baseball players and the crowd of
spectators on the bungalow steps, was ideal for my purpose. One
day I would depict the scene with Vasco peeping above the cookhouse, the next I would face round towards the Gran Sasso. Once
I showed Musso himself on the Sasso, for, although I lacked the
Primitives' innocence of vision, I shared their love of detail and disregard for scale.

The interior of the bungalows was also right up my street. The
double-decker bunks were ranged sixteen to a room, with a central
corridor that ran the length of the building, and their heavy wooden
frames gave me the structure I needed, within which to dispose the
semi-comatose and recumbent figures in the most contorted attitudes I could devise. Henry Moore's shelter drawings, familiar to me
through picture postcards from home, were doubtless an influence.

That is, I would have *liked* my figures to have the same tragic grandeur, but they usually ended by looking, merely, comic.

Like myself, Leslie had literary tendencies and had somehow acquired a *Concise Oxford Dictionary* and the *Oxford Dictionary of Quotations*, as well as an assortment of other books, which I was for ever borrowing. My ardent pursuit of education amused, also saddened, him. "I was keen on improving my mind too, to start with. I used to write the reviews of the plays and go in for essay competitions and all that. It helped take one's mind off. But when the Red Cross parcels began to arrive . . . the summer weather . . . Now I haven't the same energy, somehow. Suppose I'm a bit nuts, really . . ."

Nearly everyone, I soon discovered, believed himself to be in shocking physical condition and slightly mad. Conversations often tailed off with the refrain, "Suppose I'm a bit nuts, really," and the same man who had just walked a dozen times round the circumference of the yard at 5 m.p.h. in the midday heat, would lie on his bed grumbling that he had no energy left. Feeling perfectly fit and sane myself, I recorded—unsympathetically and doubtless unjustly—that both attitudes were a hypochondriacal effect of boredom, an atrophy of the will rather than of the tissues; certainly both seemed to vanish the minute the sufferer found something to do that really amused him. The tragedy was that, when the moment of decision arrived, the habit of inertia had grown too strong to break.

Tired of talking, Leslie offered to sit in the sun while I drew his portrait. "Not bad," he said at length, after a pause in which I held my breath—I was sensitive to comment. "It's definitely quite like me." He took it to show a friend in our room. "I say, Joe, do you recognize this?"

A big lazy intelligent man from Edinburgh, Joe passed most of the time on his bunk. Always well-dressed and groomed, he spent an hour every morning, before anyone else was up, just polishing his appearance. Now, momentarily roused, he grunted, "Um. Is it supposed to be you? Not bad." Then he sank back puffing at a cigarette holder. He was a sort of oracle, consulted by the room when there was a dispute. During the day people would come up and ask, "What's a good book to read, Joe?"; or "The Senator's offered me a packet of sugar for half a tin of Klim, but I say that half a tin of

Klim lasts longer than a packet of sugar." Joe always had a ready answer in a quiet drawling voice.

Joe's closest friend, and his counter-oracle, the Senator was an American gunner officer—so nicknamed because of his amusing accounts of corruption in his home-town politics. In the evenings he and Joe would sit for hours playing patience, discussing large issues like the state of the world or the importance of sex, and exchanging affectionate if somewhat ponderous insults.

Then there was George, a Cockney Spitfire pilot, shot down near Malta, who lay all day on a top bunk simply saying, "Aw, muck it!" at intervals. It began to grate slightly on the nerves after a while. He was always looking for an argument and usually found one with an American fighter pilot on the next top bunk. They would wrangle for hours, in shrill furious voices, about which country built the better planes. At other times they would play backgammon for matches, till that also palled. "Aw, muck it!" they would say and lie down again, while the American pilot described in detail all the girls he had, or more probably wished he had, slept with.

But there was little ribaldry of the usual army kind. The frustration and desire went too deep for joking. There had been an occasion, in one of the Musical Revues, when a Guards officer with a gift for female impersonation had appeared in a night-club sketch wearing a low-cut evening dress and jewels. The impersonation was so realistic that no one in the camp could sleep for nights afterwards and, by common consent, the performance was not repeated.

Sex was a less disturbing topic if treated statistically. On that, as on everything, Joe had the authoritative answer. To clinch an argument he was once asked how many women he thought the average man went to bed with in a lifetime. Puffing at his amber holder, he gave the question long thought before replying, "About fifty." There was a chorus of murmured protest and he looked round blandly. "You think that's ridiculous? Yes, I suppose it is; *of course* it is. Two hundred and fifty."

"Done any painting yet?"

"Not yet. Don't seem to have any energy . . ."

Kempster, to my surprise, did not share my enthusiasm for our new way of life. Hardly having seen my friends since our arrival, I was strolling round one afternoon in search of them. I'd expected Kempster, at least, to jump at the opportunity of taking up his painting career again but evidently he had been infected by the general lethargy. I found him stretched on a top bunk, smoking an Italian cigar and reading a copy of *Les Fleurs du mal*. The *shech*, which he still wore draped round his head and neck, gave him the look of an emaciated *Legionnaire* fever-stricken in some Moroccan outpost.

Sardinia had treated him and his party even more severely than the rest of us. Having marched across the island to attack an airfield that did not exist, they had been betrayed by a civilian guide sent with them from Algiers, had escaped and marched on in search of another airfield. After prodigious wanderings, Kempster himself had nearly died of malaria. I hoped that prison would help him to recover his former zest but he grumbled that he found the camp the most demoralizing place he'd ever been in.

I told him that the Art Society was holding an exhibition shortly. "The secretary asked me to persuade you to send something."

"Are you exhibiting? I saw you sketching in the yard the other day."

"Oh, I may. But I doubt if my stuff would be good enough."

"Nonsense. I should think they're only too glad of anything they can get. When is the sending-in day?"

"Not sure. I'm going to look at the notice board now. I'll let you know."

He glanced round to be certain we could not be overheard, then leant over and whispered in a somewhat melodramatic fashion, "Have you thought at all about *escaping*?"

"There's no point. I mean, we just sit and wait, surely?"

He shook his head ominously. "That's what everyone likes to imagine. I'm afraid we won't get out of here as easily as that." But the occupant of the next bunk approached and, in his normal voice, Kempster continued: "Well, let me know about the show. I suppose I'd better try to knock something off . . ."

The others, when I sought them out in turn, appeared similarly dispirited. They were watching the baseball games from the bungalow steps or just lounging on their bunks, but all had the same story. They had been glad enough to sleep at first—but you couldn't go on sleeping for ever. Now, what the hell was there to *do*? One told me that he'd been shown the tunnel. "They even have electric lamps fixed up. But they still have another fifty yards to go . . . How much longer do you reckon we'll be stuck here?"

"A month perhaps. Six weeks at most," I said cheerfully.

"Six weeks! I'll have gone nuts by then!"

Only Amos seemed thriving, as I passed by the bunkroom where he gossiped with some Guards officers he had made friends with. He waved and followed me out, saying reproachfully, "You really must come and be introduced. They're awfully nice—not in the least what you think Guards officers are like!"

"Another time—I'm rather busy just now."

The notice board gave details of sports fixtures, concerts, plays, cinemas, the meetings of innumerable societies and clubs, church services, bridge tournaments, whist drives, and Bible classes . . . I had already come to realize that no one did most of these things any longer. But Art continued genuinely to flourish and pictures for the exhibition were to be handed to the Hon. Secretary on 3rd September, the fourth anniversary of the war. I glanced nostalgically at extracts from Home Letters, then studied the Situation Report which gave no more recent news than the fall of Sicily on 17th August, four days before we arrived. A vague message that an Allied landing on the mainland could be expected hourly was the best the Camp Intelligence had been able to cook up. Our own future would greatly depend on where the landing took place. If on a level with Rome, then Kempster's pessimism could be unfounded and we might be freed almost immediately. If to the south . . . well, who could tell how soon Allied troops would reach us, or whether the Italians would have the time or inclination to move us first? There were many rumors . . . But rumors were so often no more than the echo of our own hopes and wishes.

A bugle sounded the afternoon roll-call and we fell in by bungalows with deliberate slovenliness, joking and pushing about while we waited to be counted. Or would there be a proper roll-call, a *nominale*, today? Or perhaps a search? A group of Italian officers stood in the center of the yard, while others, accompanied by *carabinieri*, carried out the check. Each bungalow in turn was called to attention, a compulsory courtesy which did not prevent everyone from continuing to talk or read. Somebody once stayed off the parade for weeks to show it could be done, another prisoner answering his name, or shifting his place quickly so as to be counted twice. Schoolboy pranks, for the atmosphere was in some ways like that of a school, rebellious against the masters and yet not daring to rebel openly.

Today the count was apparently correct. We were dismissed; and the subdued chatter that had lasted throughout changed into hubbub. Some ran back to be first in the showers. Others sat down in the dust and continued reading. Others remained in groups, discussing the latest gossip.

"One of the *carabinieri* says Badoglio has offered to capitulate if the Allies will guarantee to grab Rome before the Germans take it over."

"Bloody generous of him."

"Heard the griff? The Russians have advanced another hundred miles."

"Won't be long now. Home before Christmas I always said."

"I notice the little Commandant hasn't been on parade for a week."

"Just his way of sucking up to the S.B.O. He's shit-scared of what will happen to him when we're liberated."

"He needn't worry. Croce's the one who will get it in the neck."

"Did you see him today? Arrogant bastard. He was wearing a new uniform."

"Yes. His bitch is on heat too."

"Who is Croce? I keep hearing his name," I asked Leslie later. We were strolling together in the yard where the whole camp assembled for the last half-hour of daylight, as on a peaceful piazza, while the sunset tinged Vasco first with gold, then a deep red, and then purple.

"The camp interpreter. The tall dapper *carabiniere* lieutenant with a neat little beard and an Alsatian. He's a bastard."

Croce, I learnt, was a Fascist and the *Eminence Grise* in the camp's history. In the early days he had held back all the cables sent by the prisoners to their families—they were found in his desk by chance six months later. He had pocketed the cash for them, too. The legend of his sinister hostility had started then. The water shortage, the overcrowding, the bad cooking facilities, all the restrictions and retaliations imposed from time to time, were said to be his work and he was known to suppress official complaints which had to be made through him to the Commandant. From his curled-lip and bad-smell expression, he evidently hated the prisoners as much as they hated him and several had sworn that, when they were liberated, their first act would be to murder Croce out of hand. The threat, if he knew of it, did not appear to worry him much and after that I often noticed him striding round the perimeter wire or across the yard, for all the world like a nobleman surveying the peasantry on his feudal domain, an effect enhanced by the dog that followed always at his heels and that looked extraordinarily like a mangy wolf.

In his grey gloves, silk uniform, and well-polished riding boots, Croce cut an elegant figure as a villain—certainly one that was irresistible to the caricaturist in me. I popped both him and his dog into the foreground of the same sketch that showed Musso peering round the Gran Sasso.

"By the way, have you heard from your wife yet?" asked Leslie.

"No. I sent two or three letters from Sardinia but there was no proper P.O.W. organization there and I doubt if they ever reached her. I'm afraid I'm still officially missing. She must be worried to death, except that she's kept pretty busy, I expect—looking after the child."

The evening stroll on the yard was the saddest time of day, when people thought most of their homes, and I told Leslie a little of mine. I had been married the spring before the war, had sailed for the Middle East in January of 1940. Our son had been born in July.

"What's his name?"

"Comus." I was shy of mentioning it, but Leslie's literary tendencies helped to surmount any embarrassment.

"Milton and all that?"

"Well, a bit. Really we chose the name simply because we liked it."

"How old is he?"

"Just over three."

"And you've never seen him?"

"No."

"I'll bet you want to."

"Well, I do rather."

The melancholy mood was heightened by the song "Lili Marlene" broadcast from a gramophone record as the signal for us to go indoors. The haunting little tune was sung by a girl, which in itself twisted the dagger further in the heart. As the echoes of her voice died away and we undressed, no one ever spoke much. Then conversation in the bunkroom flared up again. George took a last crack at the American fighter pilot. But he was already dreaming of his Casanova days and George, since no argument was forthcoming, said, "Aw, muck it," and held his peace till the morrow. The Senator and Joe each lay in silence inventing some final, affectionate and unanswerable insult to fire at the other when it was too late for repartee. Polly, as always, went quietly to sleep on his own. Above me, Leslie strummed very softly on his ukulele. He was wondering, maybe, whether in the end he would ever reach Rhodesia . . .

The last joke of the night was made by Willie, an actor and the room's comedian. We lay waiting for it to come and it never failed to amuse. When silence had absolutely fallen, his voice, rich and mournful, chanted for all to hear: "Only-eighty-six-more-weeks-in-the-bag . . ."

Starting in the hundred and sixties and reducing the number each week, he had said the same thing for eighteen months every night, and every night had raised a laugh. The joke was an institution. So too was the reply of "Quiet," taken up by the room and the next one to it.

The word echoed down the whole length of the bungalow. "Quiet . . . Quiet . . ."

CHAPTER IV

"OH YES, BLACK HENS are quite different from brown or white or other colored hens," said *il professore*, smiling. "Many peasants still believe that to kill a black hen brings years of bad luck and may even cause your death. In the valley not far from Sulmona where I was born, there was a witch who cured headaches by putting the beak of a black hen into your ear. She also used the tail feathers for making spells against earthquakes . . ."

The Italian class was held every afternoon about 4 o'clock in a little room off the theater. My enthusiasm for Dante began to flag as I was forced to recognize that, even with the text and translation on facing pages, I couldn't understand, let alone appreciate, a tenth of it all. Moreover, the suspense of waiting for the next Allied move made it as difficult to concentrate on a fourteenth-century Florentine poet's vision of Hell as it had been, in our training camp a few months earlier, to take seriously Lord Beveridge's vision of Heaven. There was an end of term feeling about the class, the two or three others who had been there when I joined drifted away and after a week I had *il professore* to myself.

He was a middle-aged schoolmaster from Vasco, as different in type from Croce as could be. A friendly little sparrow of a man, his dark eyes sparkling with cynical humor and the top of his head as bald and yellow as an eggshell. He spoke nearly perfect English, having emigrated for some years to the U.S.A. in his youth, and we got on so well together that I soon dropped any pretense of learning Italian, much preferring to gossip about his homeland, the Abruzzi,

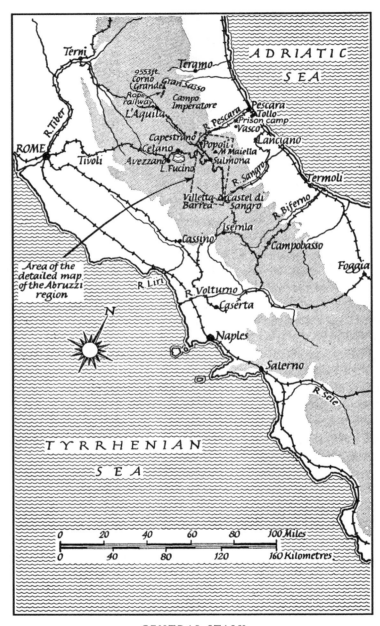

Terni

TERAMO

ADRIATIC

SEA

9553ft.
Corno
Grande
Gran Sasso
Campo
Imperatore
Rope
railway
L'Aquila
R. Pescara
Pescara
Tollo
Prison camp
Vasco

R. Tiber

Capestrano
Popoli
Lanciano

ROME
Celano
M. Maiella
Sulmona
Tivoli
Avezzano
L. Fucino
R. Sangro
Termoli

Villetta
Barrea
Castel di
Sangro
R. Biferno

Isernia

Cassino
Campobasso

Area of the
detailed map
of the Abruzzi
region
R. Liri
R. Volturno
Foggia

N
Caserta

Naples

Salerno
R. Sele

TYRRHENIAN

SEA

0   20   40   60   80   100 Miles
0   40   80   120   160 Kilometres

CENTRAL ITALY

that isolated and little known region of the central Apennines east of Rome where I so unexpectedly found myself and of which he had made a particular study. "Here round the camp is nothing," he often said. "The real Abruzzi are in those mountains you can see to the west, between the Sasso and the Maiella, and beyond."

The Greeks who colonized the ankle, heel, and toe of the peninsula, very sensibly avoided the formidable ranges on its calf. The earliest inhabitants were those Italic tribes, such as the Marsi and Peligni, who successfully defied the expanding power of Rome until subjugated in the Social War of 90 B.C. A Romano-Italic State flourished for a century or two in the Sulmona valley, where Ovid was born. As he proudly proclaimed, and as generations of school-boys struggling with the *Tristia* subsequently lamented, *Sulmo mihi patria est.*

In the next nineteen hundred years many invading armies swept through, but none stayed. There was so little to stay for. The size and barrenness of the mountains, and the severity of their winter, isolated the Abruzzi from the rest of Italy but helped to breed a long line of hermits, bandits, witches, swashbuckling eccentrics, musical shepherds, robber barons and slightly dotty saints. Flamboyant poets, I gathered from *il professore*, were a local speciality from Ovid himself to D'Annunzio. The isolation of the upper valleys also preserved a pagan culture on to which Christian Belief was early and enthusiastically grafted. To give only one example, the annual religious festival still held at Cocullo, when snakes are draped on the statue of San Domenico, certainly has its origins in a Marsi snake cult.

More sophisticated arts were practiced in the milder conditions of the plains and lower valleys. The *Abruzzesi* became renowned goldsmiths, potters, stone-carvers, and even makers of sweets. Nevertheless, the great mass of the country long remained the inaccessible haunt of wolves and bears and savage highlanders. Today the descendants of the wolves and bears are preserved in the National Park between Sulmona and Pescasseroli. As for the highlanders, their stock became mixed with that of invading Lombards, Franks, Swabians, Spaniards, and Austrians, but their attitude of bloody-mindedness to outside interference persisted—and no one has better reason than myself to be grateful that it did. For the finest product of

the Abruzzi has always been those tough, brave, independent, indus-
trious, and usually destitute peasants, whose hard way of life flow-
ered into poetry, song, and fanciful costume, and who have created
perhaps the richest folk-lore in Italy. In this century they have per-
force migrated in their thousands to the Americas, and have nearly
always returned home to die, not much wealthier than they left.

Il professore first planted in me a theoretical admiration for the
Abruzzi that experience was soon to intensify. And, as I shall tell in
due course, I have been back there occasionally since, for reasons of
sentiment, and because the region appeals to me as one of the few
places on the peninsula that have not been trodden to death by the
cultural heavy-weights. Artistically there's plenty to see, but little
that you feel all the time you *ought* to be seeing. I cannot imagine
that Ruskin or Berenson or Pope-Hennessy ever visited it. On the
other hand, Edward Lear did.

"The reason why the plots and characters in D'Annunzio's plays
about the Abruzzi seem so improbable, even grotesque, is precisely
because they are so *true*," said *il professore* on the afternoon in question, which happened to be 31st August. "You see, the country really
is like nowhere else in Italy. Until this century, it had hardly altered
for two thousand years. It is changing now, of course—but some
very queer things still happen."

We had been discussing the survival of magic and witchcraft;
or rather he had been telling me of cases from his own experience.
As a rule his stories amused and interested me, but now I found
all this talk of hens and tail feathers preposterous. How could such
an intelligent and educated man fall for such stuff? For, though
he described the cases with a certain ironic detachment, he clearly
believed that there was more to them than superstition. A prosaic
English upbringing had only qualified me to contribute a few skep-
tical grunts.

"Not all magic is done by humans," he continued. "Animals also
can be witches and make spells. Did you know that?"

"Well . . . There's one of Kipling's tales, I remember, about a
large snake in India that hypnotized monkeys and ate them. You
mean that sort of thing?"

"Possibly. I've never read Kipling. But snakes are powerful magi-
cians in the Abruzzi too. So are cats, wolves, and even owls. And

they don't use their power only against weaker creatures—they can bewitch men. Wolves are perhaps the worst. A friend of my parents, a shepherd called Giulio, was up on the Maiella once with his sheep in mid-summer. He was resting in the shade of his hut, with his dog beside him. A wolf suddenly appeared and ran round the hut in a circle. Normally the dog was exceptionally fierce, but now he just lay whimpering and trying to get up. Giulio was a brave man but he too felt paralyzed. Afterwards he swore that the wolf had grinned at him. Then it made a circle round the sheep. They remained as if stuck to the ground while the wolf killed one at a time, dragged it out of sight down the hill and came back a few minutes later for another. When the wolf had taken ten sheep, it did not reappear, but Giulio and his dog continued spellbound for a further hour."

Il professore laughed and added, "Of course it *may* have been a werewolf—we have them too in the Abruzzi, but as a rule they are only found at night. This was in broad daylight. As a boy I heard Giulio tell the story himself."

"It's a good story," I said politely, "but I don't see that it has much to do with spells. Why shouldn't there be a straightforward psychological explanation?" In those days I threw the word *psychological* into every conversation sooner or later.

"A *straightforward* psychological explanation?" said *il professore*, mocking me good-naturedly. "Such as?"

"Well, they were paralyzed with fear, perhaps. Like the monkeys with the snake. I've always heard that if you draw a chalk circle round chickens they won't walk over it. They are held there psychologically—by their own stupidity. But they aren't *bewitched*."

"Sheep certainly are stupid, and cowardly. But what of the shepherd Giulio and his dog?—remember the wolf put a spell on them too."

I did not like to suggest that they had been more cowardly than the sheep, or that Giulio had made the story up to cover himself. When I kept silent, *il professore* said, "Nowadays we depend on psychology to explain what cannot be easily explained. The peasants in the Abruzzi just put it down to witchcraft. Perhaps there are times when the two come to the same . . ."

I was still working that one out when our lesson was interrupted by a daylight bombing raid. The whole camp rushed on to the yard to cheer the glint of aeroplanes far up in the sky, heading towards the coast at Pescara, and cheered louder at the distant crunch of bombs a minute afterwards. I had rushed out with the rest, then returned to *il professore* feeling embarrassed. The fact could hardly be ignored that my people were killing his people. "I suppose they're attacking a military target, somewhere," I muttered.

He remained gravely polite. "No, there is no military target of any kind. Pescara is a small fishing port—of no importance to the war." He shrugged and added, with a wry smile, "D'Annunzio's birthplace, merely. As it happens Lieutenant Croce was also born there. His family have a large house on the coast."

"Really? I'd thought of him as Roman, or perhaps Sicilian. Well, the silly ass will hate us more than ever now, I suppose."

We'd never mentioned Croce before. Youthfully insensitive to an older man's pride and feelings, I took it for granted that *il professore*, with his obvious sympathy for the Allied cause, must share our attitude to the Camp Interpreter. Perhaps he did, but he was not prepared to hear him referred to in that sort of way. Our pleasant relationship had become cross-threaded of a sudden. He answered coldly, "No, the Croces have always lived in the Abruzzi. They are an old and important family. Their main property is in the mountains near L'Aquila. And I think you are unwise to treat Lieutenant Croce as a joke. He could do you all much harm."

"Oh, he's done that already," I persisted, my own temper rising. "The boot will soon be on the other foot."

It was a tasteless jibe, which I instantly regretted. *Il professore* brought the lesson to a close, saying quietly, "Isn't it perhaps too soon to tell?" I was afraid I had offended him but at the door he paused and, with a return to his customary friendliness, made a joke. "The *Tenente* is not so dangerous, maybe. Do you remember your Latin? *Cave canem.*" Or did he not mean it as a joke? I have often wondered.

There was no lesson the next day, but we met the day after that, 2nd September. We had hardly taken our seats when we were again interrupted, this time by an officer whom I recognized vaguely as the Camp Adjutant. Nodding to *il professore*, he said to me, in brusque military fashion, "Sorry, old boy, but could you please come and have a word with the S.B.O.?"

Like all newcomers, we had been interviewed by the Senior British Officer for a moment on arrival. Since then I had scarcely thought of myself as being, at any rate nominally, under a British military command. In fact, one of the pleasures of my present existence was the sense of having escaped altogether from the army. Still, the summons was evidently more in the nature of an order than a request, so I apologized to *il professore* and followed the Adjutant out.

He led me to a small room in one of the bungalows which I realized, with misgivings, was a kind of H.Q., with a map of the Vasco and Pescara districts pinned to the wall. The one or two other officers present were informal and friendly but an instinct warned me that something unpleasant was afoot. The offer of a cigarette, and of a glass of *vino* superior to the usual ration, quickened rather than allayed my suspicions, which increased further when Amos was ushered in and similarly entertained. "Just tell the S.B.O. they are here, will you?" the Adjutant said to one of the others, while Amos and I exchanged a puzzled glance.

The S.B.O. was a full colonel nearing sixty, with a distinguished record of service in the First World War and in India afterwards. He had been taken prisoner at the start of the Desert Campaigns and was said to have done a fine job organizing the camp in its early days, keeping up morale and squeezing privileges from the Italians. By now he was as bored with the whole thing as everyone else. He entered the room, buttoning on a military manner that no longer seemed quite to fit him.

"Got a drink? A cigarette? Good. Sorry to have dragged you both here but we have an idea which we think may appeal to you . . ." His heartiness rang a little false too.

"The balloon will be going up any minute now. It would be splendid if we could help the show on, instead of just sitting on our fannies waiting to be liberated, don't you agree?"

"Oh, splendid," we said.

"As you saw, the R.A.F. bombed Pescara the other day. We believe they're trying to destroy the bridge on the main coast road. It could be an important bridge too, if the Germans and Italians had to retreat in a hurry."

"Did they hit the bridge?"

"No—we have some good sources of information. A bridge is a difficult target from the air. A great many bombs, and perhaps lives, have been wasted. Many more are likely to be wasted—that is, unless we in this camp could blow it up ourselves."

By now it was only too clear where this was all leading. As Amos and I remained silent, the S.B.O. continued, "Of course there are plenty of chaps in the camp who would love to tackle the job. The trouble is we've been too long in the bag. We're all a bit nuts, I'm afraid, and in bad shape physically. Now you chaps are still fit. Besides, you've been trained for this sort of thing. We wondered what you'd think of the idea."

A self-respecting pirate could not very well admit that he thought it simply terrifying. It meant giving up all hope of being liberated with the rest of the camp. We'd be bound to be caught, if not before the attack, then afterwards, and would probably be shot out of hand. We asked if they happened to have any explosive, fuse wire, detonators, and so on.

"Well, no, not yet. But if you can tell us what you would need, we should be able to get it—through our civilian sources."

"Neither of us knows much about demolition," I said, seeing hope of a way out. "We were trained to place small ready-made bombs on the hulls of ships and on aeroplanes. To do any real damage to a bridge I imagine one would need at least a hundredweight. Would you be able to get that much smuggled into the camp?"

"Oh, we wouldn't want it here in the camp! You would pick it up at some rendezvous near Pescara. Those are details to be worked out. The immediate thing is to know whether you are interested in principle."

"Oh, very interested *in principle*," said Amos, who had a nice talent for deadpan irony. "What can you tell us about the bridge? Is it iron, or concrete? Single span, or with arches? Is it guarded?"

The S.B.O. looked questioningly at the others, but apparently none of them knew anything at all about the bridge, except that it existed. "I believe Mark has an old photo," said the Adjutant. It was fairly obvious that, prompted by patriotic zeal or by obscurer motives of ambition or guilt, they had hatched the plan, probably after taking too many glasses of camp *vino*, and were now pushing the S.B.O. into it.

"I suppose the civilian population would be against us?"

"Some of them might be friendly, if you were lucky, but we're still at war with their country. I think we could arrange a guide to meet you once you were clear of the camp."

"Someone trustworthy?"

"So far as you can ever trust a wop, old boy," said the Adjutant.

Remembering Kempster's experience in Sardinia, Amos and I thought we would prefer to tackle the job entirely on our own. "In any case the chief problem will be to get near the target unseen. It was hard enough in Sardinia—and that's a desert compared to round here."

The S.B.O. poured himself another glass of *vino*. "Oh, I'm not suggesting it would be *easy*. I'm glad you agree with us that it's worth attempting. There are several of your own officers in the camp. You can have them if you wish. And naturally we will do everything in our power to help from this end." He already took the operation for granted.

"How would you get us out? Have you finished the tunnel yet?"

"Not yet, but there's only a short distance to go. The tunnelers will work day and night, now there's a definite object."

After studying the map, we asked to be allowed to think it over and promised to report back the next evening. Outside in the sunny yard the baseball games were still in progress. We stood watching them, and the crowd of spectators grouped round the bungalow steps. I knew comparatively few of my fellow prisoners by sight. There were hundreds in the camp I had never even seen. Those I could see, I reflected bitterly, all looked far more interested in waiting to be liberated than in striking a blow for the Allied cause.

Amos and I were close enough friends not to pretend to be braver than we felt and the more we considered the idea the less we liked it. To escape from prison was one thing—we had ourselves already done so in Sardinia. It was quite another to make our way for a dozen miles across hostile country, pick up some explosive, locate an important bridge that would probably be guarded, pack the explosive effectively, and detonate it—and all without a scrap of previous information. Doubtless our duty was to go ahead and try. But there could not be a chance in a million of achieving more than a fillip to the morale of the S.B.O. and his staff. We felt we were being unfairly manœuvred into a position where we had either to commit virtual suicide or admit cowardice.

Before we parted, Amos said, "People are always so much more enthusiastic about the war effort when it's not their own lives they're risking. Blowing up the bridge is the sort of mad idea that Matthew Prendergast would jump at. I can't say I'm keen, but I suppose we shall have to think seriously about it."

"I shan't be able to think seriously about anything else."

Sleep came slowly that night. The girl's voice singing "Lili Marlene" had never sounded more poignant. For hours after Willie had made his joke and the cries of "Quiet . . . Quiet . . ." had echoed away, I lay awake chewing over the whole predicament. Before dozing off, I remembered that pictures for the Art Society exhibition had to be handed in the next day. I had also come to the conclusion that the S.B.O. and his staff were more than a bit nuts; they were dangerously mad. Apart from anything else it was intolerable to have my peace of mind shattered just when I was making real progress with my pen and wash technique, when I was mastering a more concise prose style in my diary, and when I had started to read an abridged edition of Frazer's *Golden Bough*.

CHAPTER V

PRISON, THEN, GAVE ME the chance to get to terms with the career I hoped to follow after the war, and on the whole have followed. It also acquainted me with something else that has been a hardly less familiar companion—anxiety.

Fear, I take it, is an expression of the will to survive, and I had come to know fear well enough. Anxiety is subtler and perhaps more demoralizing, for the issues are less tangible. It implies that a desirable state of existence is in jeopardy—a jeopardy that can only be averted by what I call creative pessimism; that is, by intense and sustained concentration, amounting to prayer, on all the possibilities of disaster and by attempting to forestall such disaster by intelligent anticipation. It may sound far-fetched to describe life in a P.O.W. camp as a desirable state of existence. However, I was enjoying and profiting by it—and it seemed doubly desirable compared with the prospect of sneaking out into the hostile countryside in a suicidal attempt to blow up an unknown bridge.

In the morning I offered the secretary of the Art Society a bunk-room interior and the sketch of the Gran Sasso, with Musso. As Kempster had predicted, he was only too thankful to receive anything, and said, "These will do fine. Damn' funny of Croce, too. The Private View will be on the sixth at three o'clock in the theater. The Commandant is supposed to be opening the show. Let me have one or two more by then, if you can. There's plenty of room."

"I'll try to knock something off," I said.

At lunch the news flashed round the camp that Allied troops had crossed the Straits of Messina and landed on the toe of Italy. We were excited, but a little disappointed. The toe was three hundred miles away and we had hoped for something more sensational. We could not know that at that moment General Castellano, on behalf of Marshal Badoglio, was signing an armistice in an olive grove near Syracuse.

Amos and I met in the yard in the early afternoon. He was much preoccupied with the prospect of playing in a cricket match. Apparently he had been a keen cricketer in his youth—he was now thirty-nine—and had been persuaded to join in by his Guards friends. I had a date in the bunkroom to draw Polly's portrait, after which I had my Italian lesson. We were due to see the S.B.O. again after roll-call.

"We'd better say that of course we're madly keen but that it will need a good deal of further working out . . ." said Amos, wincing as he flexed his arm vigorously for bowling.

"And meanwhile pray that something may turn up . . ."

We agreed on a policy of delaying tactics, and that we should offer Kempster the chance of coming, if we really had to go through with it. We noticed him strolling across the yard from the cookhouse and discreetly joined him.

"What a lunatic plan," he said, when we had explained it. "We wouldn't have an earthly of getting near the bridge and anyway none of us knows anything about serious demolition. All the same, it might be worth trying, just to escape from here. I've been taking a quiet look round and can't see any other way of getting out. The war's started—I suppose you've heard the news? If we're not careful, we'll find ourselves carried off to Germany. I was talking yesterday to one of the *carabinieri*—he told me the Germans have already grabbed some of the P.O.W. camps in the north."

"Are there any German troops near here?"

"Not yet—but there will be soon unless I'm much mistaken. So count me in if you decide to go ahead. By the way," he added to me before strolling on, "I've just handed a couple of doodles in to the Art Society. I saw your little sketches. They didn't look too bad— certainly no worse than the rest."

"Oh, thanks."

In our bunkroom a babble of conflicting opinions on the military situation continued through the afternoon while I wrestled with Polly's face. He had the rather featureless good looks that are so hard to capture and the drawing might have been the supposed portrait of a dozen others in the bungalow. But my mind was not on the work and in any case I felt more at home with architecture or figures than with faces.

To judge by the conversation round us, everyone had a friend among the *carabinieri* who had told him something different. The Germans were rushing troops down from the north, the Allies were about to seize Rome with a parachute division, the Commandant had sent for reinforcements to guard the camp . . . Inevitably, speculation on our own future was the main concern.

"The Commandant's panicking. I notice he's doubled the sentries," said Leslie. "I expect Croce is on the warpath."

"Joe, what do you think will happen to us if the Ities have to pull their troops out from here?" asked someone else.

Joe puffed thoughtfully at his amber holder. "My guess is they'll try to take us along with them. Prisoners are a commercial asset when it comes to bargaining for terms. Remember we have several hundred thousand Italians in the bag."

The Senator said, "I would question the feasibility of their moving two thousand prisoners from this camp right now. The transportation problem would be too considerable. If the Allied army advances up here at all rapidly, the Italians will be wanting every truck they can raise for themselves."

"Do you think there's any chance of them just pushing off and leaving us? Or is that hoping too much?" asked Leslie.

"Oh, there's a chance of anything," said Joe. "I suppose there's even a chance that the 8th Army might send parachutists to seize this camp and rescue us."

George, the Spitfire pilot, stirred in his bunk. "Christ, we're all wet, just sitting here doing damn' all and waiting to be rescued. We ought to try and break out on our own or something." Next to him, the American pilot snapped agreement.

Several turned on them angrily. "A fat lot of good that would do." "They'd machine-gun us before we'd gone ten yards." "The heroics-stuff is utterly pointless. One or two might escape, the rest would be worse off than before . . ."

"Aw, muck it. I only wondered what everyone thought," said George and turned over sulkily on his bunk again, the American pilot likewise.

I was surprised at the vehemence with which the others had squashed the suggestion of escape and wondered what they would say if they knew of the S.B.O.'s scheme, with the retribution that *that* would probably bring down on the camp!

"Supposing you did get away, what could you do next in a place like the Abruzzi?" said Leslie. "The peasants would catch you and hand you over at once. There's a thousand lire reward for escaped prisoners."

"Even if you reached the mountains, you'd be no better off," said Polly, more articulate than usual. "They're as steep and wild as hell. You'd die of exposure in a day or two, if you hadn't died of thirst or starved to death first."

"Surely it would depend on where the Allied line was," I said. "Food and water wouldn't matter so much if it was possible to make a dash across the mountains in, say, a couple of days."

"All very well for you," said Leslie sharply. "You haven't been long in the bag. The rest of us would be bound to collapse in an hour or two—we haven't the stamina."

"Besides, what would be the point?" said Joe. "Personally, I intend to stay quietly here till General Montgomery comes and fetches me and I advise everyone else to do the same. I don't think he'll be long now."

Il professore had not arrived when I went for my lesson. I sat trying to learn a few irregular verbs, but when, after half an hour, there was still no sign of him I joined the rest watching the cricket. Amos was bowling. He had one of those exceptionally tall and thin bodies that, in motion, acquire a grace all their own, like the grace of a heron flying. I had no idea he was so good at cricket and it was rather moving to see him now recapture this long-disused skill with such evident pleasure.

Stumps were drawn when the bugle sounded the roll-call parade. The Italians made a careful *nominale*, instead of the usual count. Afterwards Amos and I met as arranged at the S.B.O.'s H.Q. We found the Adjutant there alone. The S.B.O. had been summoned to see the Commandant.

"There's a general tightening-up, because of the news. Got any further with your plans? How many of you will there be?"

"Three at the most. We would try to find the bridge the first night, lie up near it for a day, and attack the night after. But we can't do much till we have further details of the target, explosives, etcetera."

"Quite so. One of our Intelligence staff is looking into it. Also I've contacted a Sapper officer in the camp. He can make the fuse wire and detonators from Red Cross stuff. He's a funny chap, bit of a genius in his way. You had better see him tomorrow. The explosive is the big problem. I've sent a message outside but haven't had the answer yet—I'd expected it this evening. However, I have managed to get a photograph of the bridge."

He produced a tattered picture postcard which, from the style of a motor-car in the foreground, had evidently been taken about 1925. It showed a distant view of a large iron-girder-type bridge, with at least three bays, right in the middle of a town.

"Rather close to the surrounding houses . . ."

"Yes, but by now a lot of them will have been destroyed."

"From this it looks as if nothing less than a direct hit with a 500-pound bomb would put it out of action for more than a few minutes."

"Ah, but with a retreating army piling up on the road they might be *vital* minutes. The Sapper thinks that even 50-pound cunningly placed would destroy one of the spans. He says he can give you a few tips."

"How have the tunnelers been getting on?"

"The present flap is making their work tricky but they hope to be through by tomorrow—the 4th. The 5th at the latest. So we could put you out the night of the 6th."

"Always assuming you can find some explosive . . ."

We were still sparring away when the S.B.O. returned. He was carrying a new Chianti bottle and appeared pleased with life. "The Commandant wants to stop all civilians coming into the camp. I said bluntly that I refused to run the cookhouse without help, so I think he will give in."

"Perhaps that's why *il professore* did not turn up"—and I told them about the Italian class.

They both looked startled. "That's bloody Croce. He was always suspicious of the *professore* getting on too well with us."

"Was he one of the outside contacts you mentioned yesterday?"

The S.B.O. nodded. "But we have others." And the Adjutant added, "In any case it won't affect your plan. You said you would rather work *without* a guide . . ."

They were determined to murder us.

The Sapper, whom we went to see next day, occupied the dark corner of a bunkroom and proudly showed us an assortment of inventions and experiments that, in case of a search, could be camouflaged in dried milk tins, underclothes, hollow books, and jam jars. He was the kind of technical expert who loves to make everything sound as difficult as possible. On the theory of demolition he became almost mystical, scribbling formulæ on the back of envelopes, but it was hard to tie him down to practical advice.

"In simple language, as I've tried to explain, it's all a question of thrusts," he said at length. "The photo is useless and I can't really help you more than I have without seeing the bridge. But, as a general rule, the dead center of the span is the best place to go for. If I was you, I'd dig a hole right in the middle of the road."

"How long do you think that would take?" asked Amos.

"Your guess is as good as mine. About half an hour perhaps."

"And while we were digging the hole the Italians and Germans who wanted to cross the bridge would doubtless stand quietly back and watch us?"

"No need to be sarcastic. That side of it is your headache, not mine. I'm just trying to explain the theory of the thing."

He fetched out what looked like a small Christmas pudding from under his *pallione*, opened the wrapping gingerly and revealed the contents.

"Here's a yard of fuse wire, a detonator, and a couple of time-pencils—the best I can do for you in the circumstances. Not a bad effort either, though I say it myself."

"Thanks. Good show. What's the delay on the pencils?"

"Roughly forty minutes but I can't guarantee it within ten either side. The acid is pretty ropey—I've been carrying it around on spec since Bari. But it should give you time enough to get well clear of the bang."

He wrapped it all up again. "I'd better keep this till you're ready. It could blow your arm off if you weren't careful. When do you expect to go?"

"In two or three nights—if we do go," said Amos.

"But you must go, now. Why not? I envy you. I'd offer to come myself like a shot, if I was fit."

"I can imagine," I said.

"The trouble is the old ticker"—and he thumped the region of his heart. "Not so hot nowadays, I'm afraid."

"Oh, bad luck."

"I don't grumble, but I'll be thankful to see a proper doctor. I'm on the priority list for repatriation, actually."

Again *il professore* did not appear when I went for my lesson. I'd hardly expected him to, but it gave me the excuse to visit the theater hall where the Art Society Hanging Committee had started to arrange the show, with a good deal of argument. Most of the pictures still lay on the floor and I couldn't spot mine among the few on the wall.

The secretary came up. "We all like your drawings. Have you brought us any more?"

"I'm afraid not. I've been rather busy with other things."

In fact my artistic impulses had dried up completely in the last forty-eight hours. So had the desire to improve my mind. Leaving the hall, I fetched *The Golden Bough* from my bunk and exchanged it in the library for an Agatha Christie.

Looking back, with the knowledge that it took the Allied armies nine months of grim fighting to reach the area of Vasco, the optimism in the camp at that time seems extraordinary. From the moment Allied troops landed in the south most of us really did imagine that—as Joe had put it—General Montgomery might turn up to liberate us at any minute. So much so that even the S.B.O. and his staff, who should have known better, had convinced themselves that a few hours' traffic delay at Pescara could make a useful contribution to the Allied advance.

Much of the optimism was hysterical wishful-thinking, much
was due to our own experience of desert warfare, when formations
occasionally advanced, or retreated, a hundred miles in a day. But
if we had studied a good map we must have realized that the same
kind of speed was out of the question in Italy. There were only three
routes that the Allied forces could take—up the Adriatic coast to
Pescara; along the Tyrrhenian coast via Naples and thence inland;
or over the mountains in the center. Each route was two long days'
drive in a fast car, without halts or traffic. A military formation,
spaced out against air attack and moving forward caterpillar fashion, could hardly do it in three days of non-stop driving without
the smallest opposition. No one knew how many Germans were left
in Calabria but, from the papers and from the wireless, we gathered that the Italian army, navy, and airforce were fighting the Allies
tooth and nail.

Extracts from the Italian Press, translated into English, were daily
pinned to the notice board. Their general tone, commenting on the
Calabrian landings, was a mixture of outraged indignation and sheer
despair. "We have got rid of the Fascist government. The Pope himself has made an appeal for peace. What more can we do? The British and Americans are evidently determined to annihilate us with
the full weight of their overwhelming technical superiority. There is
nothing left but to resist the invasion of our country by every means
and with our traditional valor." There was little in the press cuttings
to encourage us to expect a miraculous arrival of the Allies, nor were
they comforting reading for Amos and myself who might shortly
be at large among a local population infuriated by the bombing of
Pescara.

Nevertheless the general optimism in the camp increased hourly—
and was given a dramatic boost by an order said to have been received over the wireless direct from the War Office in London.

Amos and I first heard of this order on 6th September. We had
been keeping clear of the S.B.O., but the Adjutant sought us out triumphantly on the morning of the Art Society's show with the news
that he'd fixed the explosive. We went along to the H.Q. together,
where we found the S.B.O. rubbing his hands with excitement.

"Things are hotting up. The tunnelers will be through by this
evening and we've got 30 kilos of T.N.T. waiting for you to pick up

in a house a quarter of a mile from the bridge itself! You could leave tonight—but you may prefer to wait till tomorrow."

"We will need more time than that, I'm afraid. We've no proper boots, for one thing. There's the question of food. And decent maps . . ."

"The Escape Committee has all that laid on. Don't worry," said the Adjutant.

"Good. Well then, what about weapons? Have you any pistols or a tommy-gun?"

"Much better not go armed, old boy," said the S.B.O. "It's against the Geneva Convention. Stealth is your best weapon. Hit—and run."

"True. What happens about running? After we've blown the bridge up—or tried to. We can hardly get back into the camp . . ."

"Good lord, no."

"You'll have to make for the hills and lie up there," said the Adjutant.

"The way things are going you won't have to wait long either," said the S.B.O. And it was then that they told us about the War Office message. In the case of an armistice with the Italian Government, went the order, Allied prisoners of war at Vasco were to remain organized in the camp, pending further instructions. They must do anything in their power to assist Allied troops, but in no circumstances was there to be a general break-out into the countryside.

We asked how the message had been received, and when, but they were evasive. "Security. But it's genuine, all right. We have ways of checking that, believe me," said the Adjutant.

"They have something pretty sensational lined up, that's obvious," said the S.B.O. "A big parachute drop, perhaps. Or a combined op. landing on the coast here. It would be a terrific show if you did manage to destroy that bridge—it might make all the difference."

"Supposing our troops wanted to use the bridge themselves?"

"Ah, but if they did that, they wouldn't have been trying to bomb it, would they?" said the Adjutant.

He had us there. We agreed to return for a further consultation after roll-call, to meet the secretary of the Escape Committee.

"Keep the War Office order under your hat," said the S.B.O. as we were leaving. "It might raise false hopes. I shall be making an announcement in due course but meanwhile it's best that as few people as possible should know about it."

At the Art Society's Private View no one was talking of anything else. A surprisingly large crowd had turned up, to hear if the Commandant would have anything to say when he opened the show that might affect our future. He arrived rather late, accompanied by Croce, and made a dignified and impassioned speech. Italy had always been the most peace-loving country in the world, as her history and artistic output proved. Her treasures of painting and architecture were part of mankind's heritage; and they were being smashed to smithereens by countries that had no interest in peace, and still less in things of the spirit . . . Evidently he did not include the present art exhibition as a thing of the spirit.

Croce, the Alsatian squatting beside him, translated—or perhaps improvised—the speech sentence by sentence in a tone of such icy contempt that I half-expected someone to rush forward and strike him. There were a few angry murmurings, a few sarcastic laughs. But on the whole we accepted the harangue in silence. We hated Croce, but we could not help also admiring his arrogance and style. He may have been playing the part of a stage villain but he played it extremely well.

The Commandant and Croce did not trouble to look round the exhibition before leaving, nor did any one else much, except myself. If prison life had been an excoriating experience for the artists, their pictures did not reflect it. There were some slick charcoal portraits, a few careful life drawings, one or two crude attempts at *Punch* humor, and innumerable amateurish sketches of Vasco and its campanile among the olives. Kempster had contributed two vigorous and semi-abstract designs labeled "Baseball Players" and "Captive Fugue" in the cubist idiom of around 1910. From the usual facetious comments made they might have been unintelligible phenomena from outer space. "Which way up is it?" "I never saw anyone like that playing baseball," and so forth.

My hopes of becoming an artist after the war would depend, I felt, on how my two drawings withstood the test of public scrutiny, but I could only find the bunkroom interior, and was disheartened at how feeble and pale it looked—every bit as dreary as the rest. I had never exhibited before and experienced the terror and pride that such an ordeal entails, hovering near the picture as if in no way connected with it, eager for praise and dreading criticism. Something personal and precious was being exposed, a raw patch of my soul that any passer-by might prod. However, no one made any comment at all.

There was no sign of the view of the Gran Sasso with Musso and Croce, and I inquired after it from the secretary.

"I'm terribly sorry but some of the Hanging Committee got cold feet at the last minute. They asked the S.B.O. and he agreed that it was too controversial in the present circumstances. Would you let me buy it for two Mars bars? It will be something to take back to England as a souvenir of the camp."

"You can have it with pleasure for one Mars bar if you like it. Are you expecting to get back soon?"

"We all are. Haven't you heard?" He lowered his voice. "There's a big combined op. about to be launched on Rome, with parachute landings between here and Pescara. Any minute now . . . Well, thanks a lot for the picture. It will amuse my wife."

Utterly depressed, I left the exhibition and returned to the bungalow. I already felt a failure as an artist and it seemed probable that if the bridge plan came off I would never have the opportunity to get any better. I was lying on my bunk reading the Agatha Christie when Willie bustled in with the chocolate ration.

"Anyone want a Mars bar? By the way there's a search on," he announced without excitement. "I saw Croce and the *carabinieri* go in to the top bungalow while I was drawing these from the Red Cross stores. They won't be here for ten minutes yet."

Some kind of search was a weekly occurrence, and hardly more than a formality. The *carabinieri*, with an apologetic air, would make a perfunctory inspection underneath a *pallione* here and there, or open the odd suitcase, like bored customs officers on a train carrying impoverished English tourists. In our room, at any rate, no one possessed anything worth hiding. This afternoon, however, the search was more serious—part of the Commandant's panic. A party of *carabinieri* swept through our room and threw our things around aggressively. To my great annoyance they confiscated several of my drawings of the view from the yard, as being of possible military value.

Joe strolled in to give further news of the search. "Don't expect any more chocolate and *vino*, chaps. They've caught the tunnelers napping and made quite a haul. If you look out, you'll see them being led off to a fate worse than death."

We crowded to the window. Two dusty and disheveled officers, carrying a few toilet things and a blanket each, were being escorted across the yard towards the punishment cells near the main gate. From the bungalows their friends called out consolations and encouragement. "You're not likely to be there long." "We'll keep your cigarettes for you . . ." The officers waved back cheerfully.

The whole question of escape, and of the many ethical problems it involved, was something that the others in the room had long since made their minds up upon. Joe expressed the general attitude when he said, "Bloody fools. Serve them right." And Leslie said, "They like to think of themselves as terrific chaps, but really they're just grown-up kids—and a menace to the rest of us into the bargain. The last time they were caught we had our *vino* and chocolate ration stopped for a week."

"Hallo, Croce has caught someone else!" said Willie.

We looked again—and there was the Sapper being led across the yard by two *carabinieri* who were carrying various old jampots and Klim tins. Croce himself, the Alsatian at his heels, followed behind them. In his right hand he held what looked like a Christmas pudding in its cloth, swinging it triumphantly.

With the tunnel discovered and the detonating gear confiscated, all idea of blowing up the bridge at Pescara could safely be forgotten and I was able to devote myself wholeheartedly again to my pen and wash technique. The next morning I asked Polly if I could have another shot at his portrait. This time it was really not at all bad.

With my mind now free of anxiety, I decided to continue my efforts to educate it and that afternoon went to the library to hand in the Agatha Christie and take out *The Golden Bough* once more. The usual librarian was not there. Instead, occupying his chair and looking as if he was in the Bodleian, sat Mark Duffy, the morose don.

CHAPTER VI

IN MY YOUTH there was a First World War story about one of those hysterically patriotic ladies who distributed white feathers to anyone not in uniform. "And why aren't *you* helping them fight to save civilization?" she asked a learned-looking young man in the street. "Madam," he replied with a bow, "I *am* the civilization they are fighting to save."

The don was always armored with the same rather sardonic superiority. In the camp library I was genuinely delighted to see him again, but he looked up crossly from marking books into a catalogue, as if a tiresome undergraduate had come to disturb the college librarian, nor did he respond to my astonished and genial greeting of, "Hallo, Mark, you old sod, whatever are you doing here?"

"Oh, hallo. We met at that camp in Palestine, didn't we? I remember you quite well." He managed to infer both that this feat of memory was to his credit and that he had no particular wish to renew a contact from that chapter of his past. His appearance, within the limitations of a shirt and shorts, subtly conveyed that the pirate had been replaced by the civilized scholar. Even his bushy moustache had ceased to be the R.A.F. kind and now turned down at the corners of his mouth like A. E. Housman's.

"How long have you been here?" I asked, abashed.

"About two months."

"When were you captured?"

"I suppose it would have been soon after we last met. I was sent off in a caique on a ridiculous raid to Lesbos. An Italian M.T.B. picked us up the second day out from Cyprus."

"Who else was there besides you?"

"I was the only officer. The men were taken to a camp in the north of Italy somewhere, I believe."

"Hadn't you heard of our arrival here?" And I told him of the others.

"I think I saw—what's his name?—the one who's half-German—Kempster, isn't it? in the distance the other day, but I was in a rush to help hang the Art Society's show."

"Oh, really? I have one or two things there," I ventured, hoping to impress.

"I recognized your name on one of the drawings—I had no idea you sketched, so I assumed it was a coincidence. Which was yours? I forget."

"Well, there's one of a bunkroom. Another, of the Gran Sasso, hasn't been hung after all."

"Oh, yes, I remember the picture. I had to censor it. The situation here behind the scenes has been pretty tricky—at least for those of us who are involved in running the camp. Most of the officers are totally irresponsible, the British worse than the Yanks."

"Are you on the S.B.O.'s staff?"

"If you care to put it as grandly as that. I happen to speak Italian so I've been able to help him with various Intelligence and Security matters." All the same he made it sound as if he was virtually in charge of British Military Intelligence in Europe. But perhaps he was merely anxious to be rid of me, for he added, "The Librarian's lost interest as the result of the news. I've undertaken to try and put things in order before we hand the books back to the Red Cross—as we may have to shortly. What have you brought in? A detective story?"

"Well, yes. Actually, I came to take out Frazer's *Golden Bough.*"

"Very commendable, but I'd rather not let that sort of book out again at present, till we see what happens next. In any case I think you'd find it pretty tough going. Why not choose another detective story? There's a shelf of them over there—help yourself."

Embarrassed and irritated—the Third in History has always put me at a disadvantage with dons—I rummaged in the shelf while he fussed at his desk. A suspicion had formed in my mind, but I needed to tread warily if I was to get at the truth. The title of a tattered Penguin suited my purpose ideally and I returned with it. "Can I take this?"

"Thornton Wilder . . . *The Bridge of San Luis Rey* . . . A charming little *tour de force*." He made a note of it.

I said casually, "Talking of bridges, there's a question of possibly trying to sabotage one at Pescara."

He nodded. "Yes. It would be tricky but well worth attempting, I thought. But you shouldn't know about that. Sounds like a security leak."

"No, I was let into the secret—to give some technical advice." I sensed the absurd vanity of the man. "A brilliant idea, I thought. I wondered if it had originated with you."

"Yes, it did. One had to try and make some contribution to the war effort."

"The difficulty, it seemed to me, was getting out of the camp. They've caught the tunnelers, I hear."

He became more communicative. "Yes, but there are other ways. But I've advised the S.B.O. to keep the plan on ice for the moment, till we're sure of the next Allied move. If they get the Germans on the run up that coast road, an attack by us on the bridge might be extremely worthwhile." He continued reflectively, "The idiots in this camp seem to think they'll be repatriated the moment we're liberated—if we are liberated. Obviously that's impossible. There could be fifty or a hundred thousand P.O.W.s to cope with. But those camps that have shown some *initiative* might be given priority . . ."

"You mean, blowing the bridge would earn us a good mark?"

"Even attempting to blow it . . . Most of the other camps have been quite useless, I believe. Too windy."

"Well, it's certainly an idea. If the plan still comes off are you thinking of going on the operation yourself?"

"I wish I could. Unfortunately I'm in poor physical shape, after two months in the bag. Also the S.B.O. felt I was too much of a key man to lose."

"Yes, of course. Well, thanks for the book. Perhaps, when you've got the library under control, I can borrow *The Golden Bough* another time."

"We'll have to see." He looked up at me owlishly over his glasses and said, as I left, "I really don't think you'd enjoy it, you know."

On 8th September the evening roll-call was held as usual but the camp buzzed like a hive of bees before a swarm. The Commandant himself did not appear, nor did Croce, and only a desultory count was taken.

The text of Badoglio's communique announcing the Armistice was picked up on the camp wireless during the evening promenade. I had stayed in the bunkroom experimenting with a new technique Kempster had showed me. He had criticized my pen-line for being too thin, suggesting I tried a broader nib or the tip of a brush. The results were undoubtedly bolder and for the moment, as always when making some technical discovery, I was lost to all else and hardly looked up when Leslie came rushing in with the news.

"The Commandant has bolted and the guards have left the wire. They've produced a barrel of *vino* and there's a terrific party going on in the cookhouse. You'd better come now if you want any."

"Thanks. I'll be along soon."

My creative pessimism guarded me against premature jubilation and I was still doodling with the tip of the brush when Kempster himself paid me a visit. His attitude to the good news was also guarded. "Everyone's quite mad. They seem to think that we just sit and drink till the Allies arrive. Have you heard about the S.B.O.'s order?"

"No." The note of alarm in his voice gave me a chilly sensation and I put Art aside. "What is it?"

"No one is to leave the camp. He's had definite instructions about that from the War Office. It's fantastic. The Adjutant has even detailed an Officers' Patrol to walk round and round the wire to see that the order is obeyed."

"Well, he mentioned something about it the other day. If he really has had the order I suppose he's bound to try to carry it out. If our chaps are planning to arrive by parachute or something it's obviously better for us to stay here organized and ready."

"And wait for the Germans to come and round us up? I'm not taking any chances. I've packed some things and I shall slip out to-night—and to hell with the S.B.O. I thought I'd just let you know."

"I'll have to think about it. By the way, I thought your pictures looked awfully well in the show."

"Oh, Art!" exclaimed Kempster contemptuously. "What is it without liberty? An artist is a *man* or he's nothing. If you let yourself get taken off to Germany you will have all the time in the world for painting water-colors, but it won't help you paint any *better.*"

But Kempster had other—and better—reasons for his fear of being taken off to Germany, though it was many weeks before I learnt by chance what they were. Now he strode away, and since my enthusiasm for the new technique had vanished I joined the orgy in the cookhouse. Amos, whom I hadn't seen for a couple of days, detached himself from a group of his Guards friends. "Marvelous news and all that," he said. "I wish I could share the general hysteria. As it is I think the situation may become damned tricky. At least we shan't now be expected to blow up that bridge!"

"Don't be too sure of that" and I told him about the don. "I be-lieve Mark hatched up the whole plan intending to claim any credit for himself afterwards."

Amos, a more forgiving nature, merely commented, "A first-class brain doesn't always mean a first-class man."

Taking our mugs of *vino*, we left the throng noisily celebrat-ing and retreated to a quiet corner in the cool of the yard near the perimeter wire. The whole landscape was soaked in the deep velvety grey of an Italian dusk, to which a last ray of sunset, tipping the dis-tant snows on the Gran Sasso, added a pale and exquisite accent. Above us in Vasco the rejoicings had started. The lights were up, a rocket flared across the sky, and on the town's edge the glass and concrete hospital shone like a palace. We stood in silence for a while, sipping the wine.

"Those mountains to the west seem much closer than usual," said Amos. "I've never noticed them before."

"The Maiella and Morrone," I said. "A great place for hermits and werewolves in the past, according to my *professore*. I wonder if he'll show up again. I fancy he's been keeping clear of us, till he's certain which way things work out. I don't blame him."

"What's our best bet, do you think? Run for it or stay?"

"Frankly, all I care about is getting safely home. Of course, in a sense, the decision has been taken for us. I mean, the S.B.O. has *ordered* us to stay . . ."

"Oh, sure." We both laughed cynically and drained our mugs.

"I suppose you heard about Croce?" said Amos.

"No. Has someone murdered him?"

"Not exactly. That bag of detonators exploded while he was opening it in his office. Blew most of his right arm off. The tunnelers who were locked up heard it happen—they were telling us about it just now. They expected to be shot, in revenge. But in fact the guards were rather pleased. They all hated Croce, apparently. Said he had the Evil Eye or some such rubbish."

"It shows how much chance *we'd* have had carrying the thing through the tunnel," I said callously. "What happened to Croce?"

"They rushed him to that hospital, poor devil. I suppose he's up there now. I can't help feeling damned sorry for him. He may have been our enemy and a Fascist but you felt he was at least a *man*."

"You sound like Kempster"—and I told him what our friend intended.

"That's the gallant thing. I'm not sure it's the wisest. I don't care for the prospects either way. In fact I've seldom felt so jittery in my life—with so little obvious reason. Well, shall we go in search of more *vino*? I'd like to get really drunk . . ."

"Yes. Good lord, look at Croce's dog!"

The Alsatian bitch walked slowly past outside the wire, a few yards away. Probably she was hunting for scraps, but, before passing out of sight behind the nearest bungalow, she glared in at us with an expression of such malevolence that we both shivered.

"I saw her out there earlier this afternoon," said Amos as we continued to the cookhouse. "Just prowling round and round. One of the guards threw a stone. Savage-looking brute; obviously missing her master. If she stops out there, there's no need of an Officers' Patrol to persuade *me* to remain in the camp!"

There was no need of an Officers' Patrol to persuade anyone to remain. George and the American pilot pushed off that night, calling us all suckers. The rest of us simply stayed; Kempster also, for I met him next day in the crowd listening to the wireless news of the Salerno landings. "Couldn't very well disobey an order," he explained gruffly.

"Quite so."

It seemed certain that Rome would not now be attacked, still less landings made at Pescara. Our fate would depend on the speed of the Allied advance—and they had a long way to come. As the days passed the S.B.O.'s decision was criticized with increasing bitterness but he stuck to it, broadcasting to the camp that, since the War Office order had been definite, we must obey it till we received a counter-order. In any case the enthusiasm for a mass break-out was wholly dampened by the rumors reaching us of similar break-outs in other camps to our north. The Germans, it was said, had sent troops instantly to wherever this had happened, machine-gunning hundreds of escaping P.O.W.s out of hand, as well as any civilians found helping them.

The atrocity stories kept coming in—no one knew quite how. There was nothing to confirm them on the B.B.C. news. But they were passed round as "absolutely true."

"The man who told the man who told me *saw* it happen. The bastards simply massacred a *thousand* in an hour."

Two thousand . . . Three thousand . . .

For once duty and self-interest coincided. It was consoling to obey the S.B.O.'s order, and to blame him for it as well. You heard people saying, "I'd intended to escape that first day—if the S.B.O. hadn't forbidden it. Now it would be unfair on the others."

In fact anyone could have slipped out of the camp unnoticed any night he chose, but no one did choose, and after a couple of days the Officers' Patrol was dropped. We were as firmly rooted to the ground as the sheep in *il professore*'s story.

The nearest German division was believed to be at L'Aquila, about thirty miles to the north-west, beyond the Gran Sasso. The town had been founded by the Emperor Frederick the Second and its very name conjured the vision of a Germanic eagle, waiting to pounce. By staying quiet we prayed that the eagle would overlook us, though even the most optimistic could hardly imagine that the thorough Germans were ignorant of our existence.

Otherwise life in the camp went on with little outward difference, except that we held the roll-call parade ourselves. It provided a

break in the monotony—and a further crop of rumors. Personally, I
was relieved that I would not now be expected to blow up the bridge,
but I found I had little appetite for reading Thornton Wilder, still
less for improving my pen technique or keeping up a diary. My philosophy of staving off disaster by anticipation was being strained to
the limit—the shapes of disaster were too nebulous. So I abandoned
education and joined the rest lounging on the bungalow steps, sun-
ning their bodies and watching the baseball games. The actors and
musicians proved the most imperturbable section of the community.
The concerts and plays continued with a rather forced air of gaiety—I recall the best production I have ever seen of *The Importance
of Being Earnest* in which the don himself gave a brilliant performance as Doctor Chasuble. But this time the female impersonators
failed to set our hearts a-flutter—fear is a stronger emotion than sex.

For we were all deeply afraid, and hid our fear as best we could,
some beneath a senseless optimism, others by concentrating their
venom on the S.B.O., the most convenient scapegoat, who was now
spoken of with the same detestation that had formerly been be-
stowed on Croce.

The feeling of comradeship, of sharing a destiny, that had so
noticeably permeated the camp before the Armistice, had vanished.
Our unity was split, not, as at Athlit, into two rival groups, but
into two thousand fragments. In his heart each had only one insid-
ious preoccupation, the chances of his own safe return to England.
The closest friends grew reserved, not caring to confide thoughts
and intentions. Amos and I met occasionally to exchange notes.
We could not forgive ourselves for not having made a dash while
the going was good. Now, we agreed, it was too late. Once I visited Kempster. He also was obviously ashamed of having lost his
nerve—for it amounted to that—and lay wrapped in his *shech* in a
state of uncommunicative despair.

From the news it became increasingly obvious that the Allies
were fighting a bloody battle at Salerno and that there would be no
miraculously swift advance. On the 11th September we heard that
the Germans had taken over Rome. About the same time the Camp
News Agency picked up a London communiqué that the British
Government was still hoping for the early return of P.O.W.s in Italy
but that recent events had "complicated" the situation. Three days

later Kesselring declared martial law and gave a solemn warning to Italians who failed to co-operate or who helped escaping Allied prisoners. On the 14th, too, we learnt that German parachutists had rescued Musso from his prison on the Gran Sasso. By then even the most sanguine lost hope that there might yet be a similar Allied operation to rescue us.

Late that same night the irrepressible Willie, fresh from a triumphant rendering of Lady Bracknell, made his habitual joke. "Only eighty-four-more-weeks-in-the-bag." But for once we couldn't raise even enough spirit to shout "Quiet." The bitterness of months, or years, the dread of indefinite further captivity, the wild expectations that had seemed crowned by the armistice and that were now so swiftly evaporating, all those and a dozen other tensions had robbed us of our most valued national characteristic, a sense of humor. Indeed, the waiting had become unbearable. When, early the next morning, Leslie returned from fetching a cup of cocoa from the cookhouse and announced quietly that the camp had been taken over in the night by German troops. I felt more relief than panic.

"What fools you must be," said one of the soldiers, grinning down at us from the wire. "You've been here for a week unguarded. Why ever didn't you *escape?*"

The question has puzzled me these twenty-odd years. There is no simple, and no single, answer—nor have I intended to suggest one here. A week later a fleet of trucks swept through the gates on to the yard, to remove us to a transit camp in Sulmona, *en route* for Germany. We were given an hour to be ready. There had been three more bombing raids on Pescara in the last ten days and the trucks offered an inviting target.

The S.B.O. himself warned us of the move on the loudspeaker. It was his last public contact with us all.

"Well, this is it, chaps. We've done what we were told. We've just been unlucky."

I could not detect, in the tired crackling voice, any trace of embarrassment or guilt. Perhaps he felt none. "Why blame *me?*" he was said to have replied to a delegation of enraged American officers who accused him of having betrayed them. "I'm just as disappointed as everyone else. The War Office has let us all down."

The debacle brought Anglo-U.S. relations in the camp, always a trifle strained, to bursting point and the 500 American officers insisted on moving to Sulmona as a separate group under their own Senior Officer.

In the past day or two a curious rumor had spread, that the famous War Office order was deliberately faked by one of the S.B.O.'s staff to keep the situation tidy, and to forestall the chaos, and possible tragedy, of a mass break-out. If the rumor contained any truth I thought I could guess which member of the staff had been responsible. But whoever was to blame, the order had done no more than express what was certainly the desire of the majority, to stay put and hope to be liberated without effort. What each of us had to face for himself was the uncomfortable truth that, if we had broken out, many more of us might have reached the Allied lines, and England, than would ever do so now. We might claim it a virtue to have stayed but, as with so many virtuous actions, it was hard to distinguish between commendable self-restraint and plain cowardice.

In the bunkroom we packed with the dry-eyed despair of schoolboys at the end of the holidays, sick at heart and praying for some last-minute epidemic of measles or mumps, so to speak, to keep us at home in quarantine. The kindly tolerant atmosphere, that had so impressed me on arrival, still stayed on the surface. There was no panic or ill-temper. Willie cracked a joke. But something had gone, we were a roomful of strangers, and the indefinable bond that held us together was broken. It had started to break, perhaps, the night George and the American pilot walked out and for a week their two vacant top bunks had taunted our lack of initiative. "Serve them right if they are court-martialed," Joe had said, with quite uncharacteristic venom. (Of course they weren't. I believe they reached safety after walking 200 miles, and were even decorated.)

Poor Joe had become a discredited oracle but he remained imperturbably well-groomed, as he now wrestled to tie up four large Red Cross cartons—full of his clothing, hair lotions, manicure sets, and other treasured possessions. When it came to packing it really was extraordinary how much junk everyone had accumulated in prison. I was less encumbered and the rucksack I had parachuted with into Sardinia easily sufficed. Into it I quickly stuffed my diary, my few

spare garments and toilet things, half a tin of powdered milk, a bundle of drawings, my manuscript (from the point of view of work
accomplished I have never spent a more productive month), the copy
of *The Bridge of San Luis Rey*, and one sticky Mars bar, the price of
my Musso picture which I was saving for an emergency.

On the bunk above, Leslie couldn't decide what to carry with
him besides his ukulele. He had ten times more belongings than
would fit into a battered cardboard suitcase, acquired eighteen
months earlier somewhere along the route between Tobruk and
Bari. I helped him sort it out. "You *can't* leave the *Oxford Dictionary
of Quotations* behind!"

There is a special fascination about other people's books being
discarded. Leslie's reflected a dozen interests, taken up and abandoned. He had been for a time a keen chess-player and I browsed
in a copy of Eugene Znosko-Borovsky's *The Art of Chess Combination*. On the opening page I read these apt and consoling sen-
tences. "Absolute freedom, alas! never exists on the chessboard; no
more there than elsewhere in this life of ours. It is just a question of
degrees of constraint."

I asked him if he intended to try to escape. He shook his head,
muttering, "May as well all stick together now and see the thing
through." Outside on the yard the trucks were starting up. I had arranged to join forces with Amos for the journey, so I bade him a perfunctory goodbye. How revealing can be the unexpected glimpse we
sometimes get of ourselves in the parting words of an acquaintance.
Leslie said, "You're a secretive old bastard. I've told you all about
myself these last weeks. I know practically nothing about you."

"Perhaps there will be time enough for that in Germany."

But I somehow doubted whether there would be. The strange
peaceful interlude—that I had mostly enjoyed so much—was over,
the war had caught up with me again, and if I spent the rest of it as
a P.O.W. in Germany, it would, I vowed, be nobody's fault but my
own. Lacking Leslie's spirit of resignation at constraint, or perhaps
because I did not play chess, I yearned for absolute freedom. Besides,
I wanted to see my son. Moreover, I knew my wife would be getting
anxious . . .

The immediate question was when to try. The German troops
who had taken over the camp were a fighting formation, bored with

the assignment. Not without cause they rated us as sheep, incapable of breaking loose from the flock, and so hadn't bothered to check our numbers carefully. It was therefore feasible for would-be escapers to remain behind in the camp, hiding under beds, in the ceilings or in water tanks, and risking being tommy-gunned or grenaded if the Germans searched the camp later. Amos and I quickly discussed the pros and cons while we waited our turn to board a truck. Daunted by the atrocity stories, we felt little enthusiasm for the prospect of staying. Happily his height alone ruled out the idea.

"I really cannot go crawling under one of those bloody bunks," he said. "Let's see what Sulmona is like. It's thirty miles in the right direction. And if that's no good, there will be the slow train journey . . ."

Most of the officers had been too long in the camp to be sorry to leave it now, even though departure led to a bleaker future. "At least we shan't be seeing that view again, thank God!" exclaimed the young Guards officer, with a great quantity of black moustache and hair, whom the others called Maggie and who squatted next to me in the back of the truck as we drove towards the gates.

My own last glimpse of the town on the hillside above the cookhouse was more regretful. For the past month it had looked a little paradise, always out of reach beyond the wire but always in sight. The pantiled roofs and graceful campanile symbolized everything I longed for from life—peace, and freedom to work, and above all a civilian world geared to the changing seasons and that offered such basic delights as the sound of children, fresh bread and butter and fruit, cheap wine, and of course a wife. I only wished I could now see the smallest prospect of ever enjoying any of those delights again.

At the gates a group of German soldiers stood watching us leave. They had adopted a pet, a large mangy Alsatian dog with bloodshot eyes, sweaty coat, and its tongue panting from the heat. I only saw the dog for a second or two through the wraith of dust left by the truck in front. But I swear it grinned.

Mountains near Sulmona (photo by Emit Roma)

The Gorge of Sagittario (photo by Emit Roma)

The Abbey of San Pelino

CHAPTER VII

SINCE THE WAR I've revisited the Sulmona neighborhood twice but have always been too rushed to reach Vasco and Pescara. Besides, as two earlier Abruzzophils, the Hon. Keppel Craven and Edward Lear, both grumbled, the plain leading to the sea from Popoli is an unrewarding stretch, mainly of interest for the reverse view of the Gran Sasso and Maiella. But it was that view I wished to see again last September and the *festa* at Tollo gave an excuse to find if the camp still existed and to check a fact at Pescara.

Matthew is the sort of man who will happily walk barefoot for months across a waterless desert, subsisting on a handful of dates and occasional sip of camel's piss, but who, back in civilization, cannot endure the most trivial discomfort. He becomes frantic even if his egg isn't boiled right for breakfast. That morning, as we set off from Rome before dawn on the five-hour drive eastwards, there had been no breakfast and he huddled beside me in the *seicento* in a state of blackest gloom, whereas I, buoyed up with the prospect of the Abruzzi, felt communicative as a lark. It was still night when we passed through Tivoli where the mountains start and I told him how the King and Badoglio, after announcing the armistice in 1943, had slipped away from Rome to Pescara where a corvette took them to the Allies at Brindisi. "It amuses me to think of them racing along this same road in the small hours almost exactly twenty years ago."

"You are easily amused," muttered Matthew, trying to catch up on sleep.

He had been all for the idea of coming in Florence, but was already, I suspected, regretting it. I was only regretting having given the Abruzzi's wild beauty such an enthusiastic build-up. After all, his standards of wild beauty were so much more exacting than mine. To a man accustomed to wandering alone across the Hindu Kush, the Gran Sasso and Maiella might seem merely suburban. And how would my beloved peasants and their unspoilt way of life impress someone who spent most of the year among naked African warriors feeding off buffalo's blood?

One of the advantages of traveling with an old friend is that you know the worst in advance. A stranger's gloom can be terrifying because there is no guarantee that it will not continue for ever. Matthew's essential good temper would, I knew, recover as soon as we'd had a cup of coffee and my own was accordingly undiminished. Indeed I felt younger every minute. Dawn broke as we entered Arsoli and I said, "The Abruzzi officially start here but don't judge them by this. It's only their back approach."

"Don't think much of them so far."

The little town was still asleep but we found a café owner to make us coffee and Matthew cheered up instantly. His mood became mischievous and, seeing that I was eager to get on, he persuaded the owner to extract a second cup from the hissing machine. Holding the cup, Arab fashion, in both hands he exclaimed, "That's better. I'm sure there's no hurry to get there. Are you even certain your *festa* is today? There was some doubt."

"Not absolutely certain, but according to my old guidebook there are two neighboring villages, Villamagna and Tollo, that both have a similar *festa* to celebrate the same event. The book gives the date as the first Sunday in September so we should find something going on somewhere."

"What's the *festa* about?" he asked, when we were again on the tortuous mountain road.

"Chiefly it's about the fact that, apart from an occasional drought, earthquake, or outbreak of smallpox, nothing whatever has happened at Tollo for a thousand years. But just once in its whole history, in the sixteenth century, a band of Saracen pirates landed by mistake on the coast and pillaged the nearest inland villages. The inhabitants tricked the Saracens into part of the citadel and then wiped them out. You see, in a place like Tollo, the real enemy is boredom and they have gone on re-enacting the little victory for

four centuries. Some dress up as Saracens, the rest in period costume, and I believe the mock battle gets pretty rough. They have a
great many repressions to work off. But then, so have we all."

"Speak for yourself. *I* don't suffer from repressions!" And we embarked on the sort of argument we've been having, on and off, since
we were undergraduates, when we first began to regard one another
with amusement, exasperation, and at times dislike. The dislike
changed to affection in the war and since then we have continued
the closest friends, both accepting the exasperation as a small price
to pay for the amusement. While we zigzagged between mountains still in deep shadow I accused him of having bulldozed his
way through life and he taunted me with indulging in a hypocritical
modesty that was merely perverted egotism.

"But the whole of civilization, like marriage, depends on *someone* being prepared to give way," I argued. "I didn't want to stop
for coffee but I realized that, if I didn't stop, you'd remain in a foul
temper."

"Of course you wanted coffee. According to the rules of your
masochistic nature, as soon as you want something you have to deny
yourself it and try to place the responsibility for wanting it on someone else."

"*My* masochistic nature! *I* don't go tramping around deserts in a
hair shirt!"

"No, but you wear one nevertheless. Lucinda would agree—she
has to wash it. I say, that's rather a fine sight!

High above us the sun's early rays had lifted the sooty veil off a
peak, revealing a honey-colored crag.

"Not bad, but we'll see better. The real stuff doesn't come till
we've crossed the Fucino plain." The sky had become palest violet and the sunlit mountains seemed draped across it like sheets of
bleached and crinkled cardboard. We continued the rather dotty
tangential conversation that only old friends can have, conducted
in verbal shorthand, no sentence needing an end and where often a
single word suffices to convey a whole chain of ideas. We discussed
the mutual friends of our youth, debating why some had never ful-
filled their early promise while others had done so much more than
anyone could have dreamt. In general we deplored the corrosive
effects on them all of middle age. We speculated on what might

have become of those killed in the war and from there talked of the influence the war had had on ourselves.

"I would have thought you'd have done pretty much what you have done in any case," I said. "In fact I remember saying so once to Mark Duffy during the war."

"I'm sure I wouldn't. The war jolted me out of myself and gave me confidence. I was a pretty good mess when it started, as you probably remember. Would you deny that you gained a lot from it?"

"Certainly not. I gained enormously. Except for my family and marriage—I was lucky enough to be married before—almost everything in my life that has really mattered goes back somehow to the war." I was about to add, "Goes back to the Abruzzi," but he had started on a favorite theme, the lack of any real challenge facing the young men of today. "They need to test themselves, but what on earth *is* there in the present age? No wonder they roar round on motorbikes and get into trouble. In their place I'd do just the same!"

And we flogged that topic through Tagliacozzo and until we descended to Avezzano, which proved as noisy as only a modern Italian town can be on a Sunday morning, with most of the population revving up their scooters and Fiats for a day at the sea. Matthew suggested another coffee. He has an insatiable craving for coffee—a hangover from his Bedu period.

"Yes, a good idea," I agreed.

"You'd *really* like a coffee or are you just saying that to be civilized?"

"No, I'd really like one."

"Talking of being civilized," he said, when we started off again, "Mark Duffy's another person who's never really developed, don't you think? I mean, all that intelligence and knowledge. And then to become a television personality!"

"Who's hypocritical now? I watched you being interviewed on the telly not long ago and you adored every minute."

"Well, it was rather fun, I admit. Just once. But I'm told Mark makes a habit of it. We overlapped for a year at Oxford. He was quite brilliant. I forget if you knew him then?"

"No, I only came to know him in the war. At that Athlit camp, actually. Then later . . . There's a good deal to be said for Mark. He wrote to me before I came to Florence but I haven't seen him for years."

We had started to cross the Fucino plain, so fertile and so dull. It was a large lake till a hundred years ago and I described the many attempts to drain it, beginning with the Emperor Claudius's failure and ending with a Prince Torlonia's success. "It cost him a fortune—and made his family an infinitely greater one in the end. The effect on the wretched local peasants is the theme of Ignazio Silone's *Fontamara*—which might well be that village over there."

But Matthew was gently snoring. I let him sleep, as we climbed at length into the country of the Marsi, that strange race of snake-charmers whom legend connects with Circe's son Marsius; or with the unfortunate Marsyas? But the possibilities of ignorant speculation are endless and as Keppel Craven, most polysyllabic of travelers, comments, "It would therefore be superfluous, as well as tedious, to enter into a detail of the learned controversies."

A mile or two beyond the summit of the range I drew on to the verge and halted. "Wake up," I said, "this is what I've brought you to see."

We got out and stood poised like eagles, gazing far down into the valley where the rivers Aterno, Gizio, Sagittario, and a few smaller streams converge near Popoli, to become the River Pescara that flows out through a gorge to the Adriatic plain. The great mass of the Gran Sasso framed the valley to the north, thunderclouds dispersing over its two snowcapped horns in doodles and blobs like a vast Alexander Cozens water color. To the south, the valley ended with the Maiella and the barren hump of Mt. Morrone, below which I could just see the glint of Sulmona. Ovid somewhere describes the same view, returning with a friend for a quiet spell at his country home after the fevers of Rome. The details of the scene can hardly have changed in 2000 years, except that in his day there were more trees on the mountains and he would have looked down on to the extensive roofs of Corfinium, the capital of the province. All that remains of it is a fragment of wall, near the magnificent ruin of the Romanesque abbey of San Pelino.

There are dozens of views that are more intimately woven into my life, that I know and love better. Folds of the English downs, cor-

ners of London or even of Florence, the view from this studio window in Surrey where I write, with its pigsty under a chestnut tree.
But none can affect me in quite the same way as the view, from any
direction, of the Sulmona Valley. The dramatic contrast between
the fertile plain and the utter bareness of the enclosing mountain-
sides; the little railway from Roccaraso, winding over viaducts across
Monte Rotella; the hint of beech forests high in the upper reaches
of Monte Genzana; the very smell of the cultivated earth, whether
parched to grey dust or darkened by rain to a deep red—all fill me
with an almost painful longing, and carry me back to the ten weeks
in my life when, though often starving and in great fear, I was probably most intensely *alive*.

I could hardly expect Matthew to share the nostalgia that over-
whelmed me and I glanced anxiously to see how he was taking it.
He was smiling a little and said quietly, "Yes. It was certainly well
worth coming just for this."

The rest of the day was an anti-climax.

A stream of trailer lorries spoilt our descent into the valley and
at Popoli we joined a noisy queue of traffic heading for the sea at
Pescara. We entered the gorge and I said, "How well I remember
coming through here on our way to Sulmona from Vasco. We were
packed into open lorries and Amos and I kept wondering if it was
worth jumping out but, as you can see, one would not have had
much chance."

At last I spotted Vasco itself on a hill to our right. It had changed
to a sprawl of modern buildings, even the campanile was new, and
bore no resemblance to the town that I remembered as a little paradise. In my anxiety to identify the camp I grew careless and had to
brake hard to let a sports car squeeze in front of us.

"For Christ's sake!" exclaimed Matthew, putting a hand against
the windscreen.

"He cut in. If I hadn't braked he'd have hit that oncoming lorry."

"The whole of civilization depends on someone being prepared
to give way . . . Your *festa* will have to be damned good to compen-
sate for all this."

"I do believe those are the gates, where that sentry is," and I
pulled in to the entrance of a dusty Italian barracks, opening on to

a large parade ground surrounded by bungalows. "That's it all right. Twenty years since I left, to within a week or so." I was hoping for some sort of kick but felt nothing at all. "Now we're here, I must just take a glance round."

"When I wanted to stop for coffee at Popoli you said there wasn't time."

"These *festas* always start late and if I leave it till this afternoon the Italian army will have gone to sleep. Please be patient. After all, I look back on this camp as the turning point in my life."

Matthew became slightly more interested, if only in the idea that my life might ever have had a turning point. We approached the sentry, who fetched a corporal, who fetched a lieutenant who, in turn, fetched a grizzled and suspicious colonel. Yes, he knew it had been a P.O.W. camp but it was his barracks now. He had fought against the British in Eritrea, he said, and obviously saw no reason why he should be bothered on a Sunday morning with a couple of untidy specimens of the race whose Italian he could hardly understand. For a moment it appeared hopeless, but there is an *Abruzzese* proverb:

> *Una bugia ben detta*
> *Val piu di un fatto stupido.*

A plausible lie is better than a stupid fact. I told him we were two British generals going to a N.A.T.O. conference in Rome and that did the trick.

The dusty yard had been planted with oleander, the bungalows spruced up with green and yellow paint. Otherwise, except for the lack of baseball players, it all looked much as before. Vasco still peeped above the cookhouse but now the view lacked charm. In the other direction a heat haze hid the Gran Sasso. The *tenente* who showed us round had only the vaguest notion of the war. He had been born in 1942. We felt very old.

"Well, I hope it was worth the trouble of seeing it again," said Matthew as we rejoined the traffic stream.

"It tidies things up in my mind, at least. By the way, did you notice a large Alsatian dog by the camp gates as we left?"

"No, I didn't see any dog."

"Perhaps I imagined it."

We by-passed Pescara, branching south along the coast road and then, five miles farther, turned inland. Tollo appeared to be a dusty ordinary little village, mostly rebuilt since the war. There was no sign of a *festa* and no one much about. The owner of the only café we could find said that the *festa* had taken place, as usual, on the first Sunday in *August*. Idiotically I had mistaken the month.

"I don't think you would have enjoyed the *festa*—it's not for tourists. This year one of the Saracens had all his teeth knocked out." He shrugged his shoulders, explaining that the villagers became a little over excited. He had lived for years in America, and could hardly wait to return there. "Tollo is a very dull place compared to Seattle. You've been to Seattle perhaps?"

We regretted that we had not.

"I don't know much Italian but I do know the difference between *Agosto* and *Settembre*," chuckled Matthew, as we hastened back along the road from Tollo. He was in boisterous spirits at my discomfiture.

"Well, I'm sorry and there it is. I can't go on apologizing. Perhaps everything is for the best. We'll lunch at Pescara—I wanted to call in there anyway. And we shall have more time for Sulmona and my peasants."

"Are you sure they haven't all gone to Seattle?"

"Quite sure. One of them has been in Boston for ten years but he's now back."

The day had become uncomfortably hot and the coast road was as noisy and overcrowded as Viareggio. Matthew kept saying gleefully, "You won't be allowed to forget this in a hurry! Bringing me to a place no better than Southend to watch a fancy dress battle that had happened a month before . . ."

"Your sense of humor is basic," I said. "I suppose that's why you get on so well with savages."

The problem would be to find the information I was seeking. On a Sunday the library, town hall, or other places of reference would be shut. Pescara, almost entirely demolished by Allied bombs, has been rebuilt on a far larger scale. We drove across the wide modern bridge under the impression that it was part of the main street. I pulled up at a bookshop that was selling postcards to tourists. Matthew settled himself in a coffee bar next door, while I went in. The owner, a man of about fifty, had always lived in Pescara. Pictures of the town before the war? Well, that might be difficult. Everything had been destroyed by the bombing. He believed he still had a few copies of old postcards in an album somewhere and I accompanied him to a back room.

Yes, of course he remembered the bridge, if I meant the *Ponte Littorio*. He even remembered it being built in 1933. First they had demolished the old iron girder bridge and put up a temporary wooden one. The *Ponte Littorio* of course had been in solid concrete. They were very proud of it. Had it been bombed? Oh no. The bombs had all missed. In the end the Germans had blown it up with mines before they left in June 1944.

He couldn't find any postcards but he did better than that. He produced a little handbook on the *Ponte Littorio*, published to celebrate its opening in 1935 and with an architectural drawing that gave dimensions. Four concrete piers, each four meters wide, supported three concrete arches. Each arch was 2 meters thick at its thinnest point. The bridge was 106 meters long and 18 wide, with four bronze eagles on columns and four allegorical female figures representing the mountains, the sea, the river, and the countryside . . .

I asked if I could buy the book. Well, it was not worth anything exactly. More of sentimental interest. Why did I want it?

"I have a friend in England," I explained. "A distinguished professor, an expert on military history. I am so anxious to send him this—you see, he once had the idea that this bridge could be destroyed with thirty kilos of T.N.T."

I don't suppose he understood a word but, being a courteous Italian, he insisted on my having the book for nothing. He even wrapped it up and undertook to post it himself to the address in Oxford that I wrote out. At least he allowed me to pay the cost of the stamps.

CHAPTER VIII

MT. MORRONE towers above Sulmona somewhat as Mt. Hafelekar above Innsbruck, with the differences that Sulmona, much battered by earthquakes, pestilence, and war, is smaller, more austere and less modernized, still keeping its medieval-walled shape, and that Morrone, from a few hundred yards away, seems as destitute of all life and vegetation as a sheet of parchment. Actually the brown rocks, rising sheer from the valley without vineyards and olives to soften the transition, are finely carpeted with aromatic scrub and wild flowers, while a million cicadas hum like a hidden dynamo.

The barrenness of the mountain greatly accentuates the lush effect of the plain. Ovid, in exile on the Black Sea, wrote nostalgically of "cool Sulmo" and its "ice-cold streams." One of the streams, the Vella, flows just north of the city walls, the Gizio just south, and his description in the *Amores* of trying to cross the Vella's muddy reed-fringed banks, impatient to reach his mistress Corinna, is still recognizable. The dusty track leads after a mile or two to his Fountain of Love, presumably also much the same now as then with women slapping clothes on the stones, and from there on up to his villa on the lower slope of Morrone, at any rate to the ruins of a large Roman building known as such.

Ovid continued as a living force in the Sulmona neighborhood for nineteen hundred years, a legendary hero-scapegoat, the local squire's son who went off to Rome, became the friend of the Emperor, and was then mysteriously banished, no one knew, or still

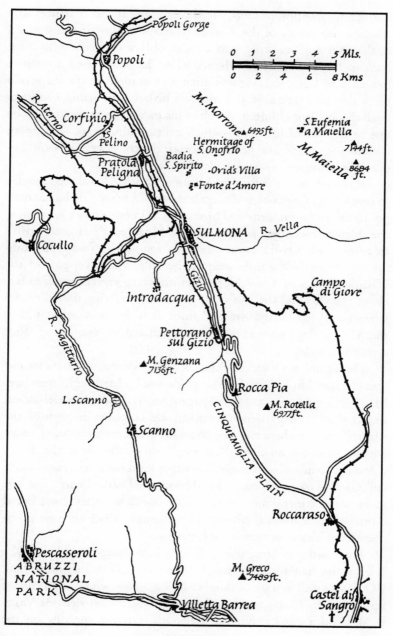

Póopoli Gorge

Popoli

0 1 2 3 4 5 Mls.

0 2 4 6 8 Kms

R. Aterno

Corfinio

M. Morrone
▲6495ft.

S. Eufemia
a Maiella

S. Pelino

Hermitage of
S. Onofrio

7144ft.

M. Maiella

Pratola
Peligna

Badia
S. Spirito

•Ovid's Villa

8684
ft.

Fonte d'Amore

SULMONA

R. Vella

Cocullo

R. Gizio

Introdacqua

Campo
di Giove

R. Sagittario

Pettorano
sul Gizio

M. Genzana
7136ft.

Rocca Pia

M. Rotella
6977ft.

L. Scanno

Scanno

CINQUEMIGLIA PLAIN

Roccaraso

Pescasseroli

ABRUZZI
NATIONAL
PARK

M. Greco
▲7489ft.

Castel di
Sangro

Villetta Barrea

ABRUZZI

knows, why. Appropriately, in the land of snake-charmers and witches, the author of the *Metamorphoses* was himself transformed in the course of centuries into a sinister black magician who came back to haunt the neighborhood, where he had buried a treasure (which is still dug for). He was often seen at night in the shape of a black dog or a werewolf and mothers invoked the name *Uiddie* to quell disobedient children. Much of his magic power was said to be due to the size of his nose—which endears him to me, having an outsize one myself, and he could absorb the contents of a book simply by standing on it—which alas I can't.

In the Abruzzi the mythical Roman and Medieval past are not so remote, if often confused together. Legend made Ovid a contemporary of, and even identified him with, Sulmona's other great man, the thirteenth-century hermit Peter of Morrone. Peter used Ovid's treasure (with Ovid's connivance) to found the Badia of Santo Spirito, about half a mile west of the villa. His cave, part of the Hermitage of Sant' Onofrio, perches on a crag several hundred feet above the villa and the half-crazy old man was living there in 1293 when the Papal envoys dragged him off to be crowned as Celestine V—the Pope whom Dante anathematized for renouncing office after six months.

The legend of Ovid, the Badia of Santo Spirito, and the Hermitage of Holy Humphrey (as the guide-book charmingly translates it) . . . Examples of tenacious paganism, redundant ecclesiastical foundations, and extreme asceticism are common enough in the Abruzzi, but nowhere else can boast such fine examples of all three within so small an area. Beneath Ovid's villa, near the Fonte d'Amore, stands a monument of another kind entirely, a ramshackle collection of barrack huts enclosed by tattered barbed wire. The barracks are not mentioned in the guide-books but they contributed a brief chapter to local history. In September 1943 we were taken there from Vasco, in transit for Germany.

The warren of bungalows, divided into compounds by shabby brick walls, had accommodated three thousand British other rank P.O.W.s, as well as a small number of Yugoslavs, who had all rushed up on to Mt. Morrone when Armistice was announced. At Vasco we'd heard a rumor that the Germans, arriving speedily on the scene, had mown them down wholesale. In fact, as we now learnt, the Germans had shown considerable forbearance, climbing the mountain in pursuit (and it is a grueling climb as the Papal envoys found at the same season), firing over their heads, and shouting at them through megaphones to return. Two thousand had been recaptured, or had been driven down by hunger, thirst, and exhaustion, and were penned up in one of the compounds. The remaining thousand were still at large on the Maiella, requisitioning food from the shepherds who, in September, had not yet left the high pastures with their flocks. Their abandoned possessions littered our part of the camp in a dreamlike chaos, the bungalows and spaces between being piled with broken beds and torn mattresses, with decomposing books and magazines, with old clothes, Red Cross stores, cooking utensils, and indeed every conceivable object, like a gigantic refuse dump outside an Italian village. For the first few hours the pleasures of scavenging did much to raise our dejected spirits.

On the first night the 500 U.S. officers, who had stayed firmly together, discovered a hole in the perimeter wire and about sixty of them slipped through before the guards saw what was up and started firing, but only one American was wounded. Thereafter the Germans brought further troops to surround the camp. By day patrols were stationed half a mile out, closing in by night with machine-guns on fixed lines. The wire itself was overhauled. Odd individuals continued to try to get through each night but none succeeded. Effrontery was more successful than stealth. One British officer, wearing running shorts and gym shoes, walked briskly out of the main gates in broad daylight. Five others, with a sixth dressed in an improvised German uniform, also marched unchallenged past the guard who mistook them for a fatigue party. By bad luck they bumped into a patrol at the Fonte d'Amore, and were personally congratulated by the German Commandant before being shut in the cells.

Group solidarity had got us nowhere and by now, even the most scrupulous conscience agreed, it was every man for himself. We realized that we had been deluded less by the S.B.O.'s order than by our own imaginary fears. There had been no massacres. The Germans had not even searched the Vasco camp after our departure and the dozen or two bold spirits who had hidden must already be far on their road to freedom. Well, we wouldn't let ourselves be deluded a second time and were seized by an escape-mania as futile as the earlier lethargy. At Vasco we had been passive as sheep, at Sulmona we became as busy as beavers, and the whole camp echoed to the sounds of excavation—wherever Ovid's treasure may be it's not there. Old beds were broken up to be used as trap doors and pit props and soon there wasn't a plaster ceiling that had not been burrowed into, the hole camouflaged with pin-up photos. The Germans had our numbers short by thirty and at the daily roll-call thirty of us stayed off parade. But it began to be obvious that if *everyone* carried out his private escape-plan the camp, when the day came to move, would be virtually empty.

After the Vasco debacle the S.B.O. and his staff gave up trying. Centralized government was discredited and, like Anarchists, we managed quite well without. We organized ourselves in messes of about a dozen, drawing a basic ration from the Germans and titivating it, or supplementing it, as best we could. Amos and I shared a little room with his friends from the Guards, civilized companions whom I regretted not having got to know better in the more expansive conditions of Vasco. They had had the foresight to ransack the library and, when not excavating, we exchanged books or lay around pleasantly gossiping. Six of them were digging a hole in the concrete floor, the entrance hidden with a bed. Others, more philosophic, preferred to leave their fate to chance. One, who had loathed the army, made no bones about hoping to be taken to Germany. "I had begun to act quite well at Vasco. It seems a pity to give it up now." He had my entire sympathy.

The Vasco wireless sets had had to be abandoned but the war news was not the less optimistic for being speculative. The Allied line stretched from Naples to Foggia—and of course was advancing over the mountains at a gallop. With luck there would be no time to move us. The same thought had occurred to our guards who were rather amused by the frantic digging activities, of which they were perfectly aware. "Why are you worrying?" said a sentry, coming unexpectedly on an officer emerging from a hole in the floor. "It's *we* who should be worried!"

By this stage the Germans were not in the mood to chase up the mountain after anyone. They let it be known that they intended to tommy-gun all the ceilings before departure, and then set fire to the huts. After that the sounds of excavation noticeably diminished.

"The trouble with cooking as a rule is that there are too many ingredients to choose from," said Amos. "Try some of this boiled biscuit—it really isn't unlike porridge. And here's some grated chocolate to sprinkle on it."

With a little imagination and goodwill one can pretend to enjoy eating almost anything, even the food supplied on British Railway stations. And, to please Amos, I agreed that the meal, which he'd spent a happy hour preparing, was delicious.

"The simple life for me," he continued. "My own, I realize, has always been too complicated. Possessions only lead to debts and worry."

We planned to stay behind in the camp—I, for the reasons stated, Amos, simply for the hell of it. Our first attempt at a hideout was in the ceiling of a derelict bungalow. We were busy tearing up a bed and passing the pieces into the roof to reinforce the plasterboard, when we were stopped by an indignant British C.Q.M.S. belonging to the original camp staff. To our amazement he was concerned for the damage to barrack stores, as though we had all been in Aldershot! Bitter recriminations followed on both sides. But in any case our hole was compromised, so we began instead to dig a slit-trench outside our own room. The ground was rock hard, our work frequently interrupted by German sentries, but by the end of a week we had finished it and improvised a wooden lid, camouflaged with earth and a tomato plant.

There was no piazza on which to meet one's friends of an evening—the parade ground was just outside the wire and we only assembled there for roll-calls under guard. Busy with my own affairs, I saw nothing of Leslie, Polly, and my other room-companions from Vasco, though once I passed Joe, well-groomed as ever and with the amber holder in his mouth, scurrying along, like myself, with a Red Cross carton full of earth.

Another time I visited Kempster, whom I'd heard had gone to ground with the Yugoslavs, disguised in their uniform. The disguise suited his dark good looks so well that I only identified him by the *shech* which he still wore. His rubber-soled parachute boots looked odd with the dark grey puttees and knickerbockers. He was sitting in a hut, talking German to a dark-haired Yugoslav of his own build and was clearly not pleased to be visited, indeed went through a rigmarole of not knowing who I was and offering to help me find whomever I wanted. He led me to the shelter of a wall, and, after making sure we could not be seen either by Yugoslavs or by German sentries, explained tersely that his escape plan required complete secrecy. "The situation is trickier for me than you can understand. Whatever happens, I won't let myself be taken to Germany." Indicating the uniform, he added, with a bitter laugh, "I suppose this shocks your conventional English public schoolboy soul?" I was annoyed with myself to recognize that, as a matter of fact, it did.

The Germans, for some vindictive reason, gave the Yugoslavs less food than the British and Americans, and Kempster was clearly half-starved. I offered him a few cigarettes and my Mars bar, which by now had melted to a tacky mess. Before we parted he scribbled down the name and address of his younger sister on a scrap of paper and asked me to contact her after the war—if things worked out that way round. The name was Italian, the address in Florence. I gave him my wife's address in England and—rather self-consciously—asked him to do the same for me. To my conventional soul the exchange smacked too much of a hundred similar incidents in books and films. Then we wished one another luck and shook hands—and that was the last I saw of Kempster.

One morning, when we'd been in the camp a week, Mark bustled in to our room. The only member of the S.B.O.'s former staff who still attempted to organize anything, he had become the unofficial camp Adjutant, and had visited us once or twice to relay orders from the German Commandant. Now he was on a mission for the Americans. When the move came, they intended to remain together as a body and had hatched a wildly ambitious project to commandeer the whole train and drive it south towards the Allied lines. They had asked him to pass the word round discreetly—to avoid misunderstandings.

Amos, who was preparing a broth with three mouldy potatoes found in a decayed mattress, invited Mark to stay for lunch. "Extreme simplicity is the hallmark of a great cook. Try some Sulmona soup."

But Mark took one sniff at the stew and declined.

The order to move was given suddenly on 30th September about
1 P.M. The British officers and Yugoslavs were to parade immediately on the space outside the camp, where lorries had begun to
arrive. The British other ranks and the Americans would follow the
next day. In our room the six officers scrambled down into their
hole and we pulled the bed into position over them. The rest gathered up their belongings and, with a gallant attempt at cheerfulness,
bade Amos and myself goodbye. They had ceased to care very much
where they went. Only the budding actor appeared eager to reach
a destination where he could practice his talent. (Long afterwards I
heard that he had gone from strength to strength in a P.O.W. camp
in east Germany—and had been accidentally killed in the last few
days of the war by the liberating Russians.)

While Amos and I discussed our next step, we stood inside the
doorway of the hut watching the rest assemble on the parade ground.
Like truant schoolboys, the pleasure of getting off something was
marred by a considerable funk at the possible consequences. The
lorries could only ferry a hundred at a time to Sulmona and the
move would last all afternoon. For the present the Germans weren't
bothering to patrol the inside of the camp. They needed all their
spare men to check the numbers on parade and to escort each batch
sent off to the station. If we decided to stay hidden, our slit trench
could only accommodate one of us. The other would have to find
somewhere else. But neither of us relished the idea of being caught
in the camp when the final round-up began. It might be best to try
to get through the wire the same night; or, perhaps, gain a day's
respite by joining the other ranks?

We removed our badges of rank and slipped across to their compound, where we recognized a good many other officers with the
same idea. But sooner or later, as we knew, the other ranks' numbers would be checked, the discrepancy noticed. The other ranks
knew this too. "Here, you two don't belong here. Piss off!" said the
same C.Q.M.S. we had fallen out with already. His comrades supported him and, with such dignity as we could muster, we did as
they instructed.

Back in the officers' part of the camp a few other figures flitted among the huts. It was 3.30 P.M., a time when the Italian sun,

though lower in the sky, often seems hottest. From that, or from the tension of waiting, I had a blinding headache and privately cursed the whole idea of escaping. There were still three hours of daylight. We had better hide till dark at any rate. Amos settled down in the slit-trench with a book and I covered him over with the wooden lid, scattering dust on top and placing the tomato plant as naturalistically as possible. "Are you O.K.?" I called, dubiously, and was reassured by a muffled answer, "Quite O.K. And there's enough light to read by."

Courage is often only a matter of high spirits, of feeling *well*. I felt terrible, and longed, merely, for a couple of aspirins, a glass of cold water, and a pair of soothing sheets on a comfortable mattress. In their absence, I crawled behind a stack of broken beds in one of the deserted huts, conscious that my feet could easily be seen by anyone stooping to floor level, but lacking the will to search further. I slept for an hour or two—and was woken by a familiar voice shouting, from the other side of the beds, "I can see you in there, whoever you are. For God's sake have some sense and come out. There's a crisis."

Feeling foolish, I crept out on hands and knees.

"Oh, it's you," said Mark. "It would be."

The move, I learnt, was still in progress but the Germans, realizing that the number of British officers would be at least two hundred short, had summoned both the S.B.O. and the Senior American Officer and warned them that unless the missing British appeared within half an hour the deficiency would be made good from the Americans. The strain on Anglo-U.S. relations became acute. When they were alone, the Senior American Officer told the S.B.O. that the loss of 200 would wreck their plan to seize the train. They were damned if they would be let down by the British a second time— it was up to us to produce our own men. And so forth. Mark, and a few other public-spirited individuals, were scouring the camp to persuade as many of us as they could find to uphold the national reputation for fair play. "The whole of civilization depends on *some-one* being prepared to give way," he argued.

I was only too prepared to give way—my headache was worse than ever. Amos, when I had uncovered him and explained the predicament, agreed, with a grin of relief, that our duty was plainly to help the Americans. He had been in his grave for three hours and, though none the worse, was not sorry to rise from it. We collected a few things from our room and shouted the news to our six friends under the floor, but they decided to remain where they were.

"The great question," said Amos as we jolted towards the station in the back of a truck, "is whether the natives are friendly or hostile. I mean, if we did manage to escape, would the local peasants help us or hand us over instantly?

"Why, after all, *should* they be friendly?" he went on. "We've destroyed their armies, bombed their cities. Now we're trampling their country underfoot. They have little enough food for themselves, I imagine. And if they're caught helping us by the Germans they'll be shot. If you were them would you help us?"

I replied, weakly, that I certainly would not.

The truck halted suddenly at the Fonte d'Amore, to take on board a bedraggled British officer who turned out to be Joe. He told us he had jumped unseen off an earlier truck and had lain for half an hour in a muddy irrigation ditch until spotted by a party of peasants working in the fields. They had proved themselves very unfriendly indeed and, with much abusive shouting, had been leading him back to the camp when we passed. So that answered Amos's question.

"At least we now know how we stand," he muttered. "All men are enemies."

The station, when we reached it, seemed to have been dipped in vermilion. A flaming sunset lit the twin peaks of the Gran Sasso in the far distance. Just across the valley, the Hermitage of San Onofrio showed up as a pale pink scar against the purple mass of Mt. Morrone and to our immediate south a few shadowy towers and campaniles peeped above tree tops.

"You know," said Amos, "Sulmona might be rather a jolly sort of place to spend a honeymoon in peace time."

Shepherded by sentries, the long queue of prisoners shambled forward a few yards at a time in the dust beside the line towards a train of cattle trucks. As darkness fell, a row of lamps, partially blacked-out for fear of bombing, threw a ghastly half-light on the queue at intervals. My headache grew so severe that, when possible, I squatted on my rucksack. I must have looked as ill as I felt, for I

remember a German soldier coming up to ask, with strange solicitude, whether I needed a doctor. Thinking of cool sheets in a hospital I was tempted to say I did, but Amos assured him that I was
all right.

Laughter and shouts of greeting in the rear of the queue heralded the arrival of the remaining officers from the camp. In the
end all had been persuaded to do their duty by our Allies. Our six
friends wandered up. "We decided to pack it in in any case," said
one. "We'd overlooked the ventilation problem. In fact we hadn't
enough strength left to push the bed off. So we simply shouted and
a passing German let us out!"

Mark, finished with staff duties, also joined us. He and Amos
began to speculate on our route to Germany. At Sulmona the mountain railway that has wound its way up from Roccaraso and Isernia
in the south splits into three. One line goes west to Rome, climbing into the Marsi hills past Cocullo (of the snakes). Two further
lines lead north, one to L'Aquila and on across the Apennines, the
other turning east at Popoli to join the main line at Pescara. It was
unlikely that we would move all the way back to Pescara. Rome also
seemed improbable.

"We'll go via L'Aquila I expect," said Mark.

"Perhaps Croce will be waiting there to say hallo," said Amos.

"The German Commandant told me yesterday that he'd heard
he had died in hospital."

From somewhere at the head of the queue a shot rang out. The
shuffle of feet, the subdued murmur of fifteen hundred-odd voices,
changed abruptly to an eerie silence that lasted a few seconds. One
or two shouts, then silence again, and then the conversations started
up with forced unconcern.

"One of the Yugoslavs made a dash for it. A sentry shot him
dead."

The message, whispered back along the line, added an extra chill
to the night air. "I saw it happen," said a voice near me, later. "A big
dark chap, with a sort of white cotton scarf round his neck." Later
again, we filed past the dim shape, a pair of boots protruding from
under a sack, a warning to anyone who might be contemplating a
similar dash. "This is all just a bad dream," I said to myself over and

over again, fingering the scrap of paper in my pocket with Kempster's sister's address. Then I was quietly sick.

Some time after that, around 11 P.M., Amos, Mark, and I squeezed into a cattle truck with thirty others. The floor reeked faintly of sheep, or it may have been goats. The sliding door rattled shut and was bolted from outside. Once used to the dark, I could see a glimmer of sky through an open ventilator under the roof on the opposite wall. Soon afterwards the journey to Germany began. For a while we shunted forwards, then backwards. Half-dozing I wondered if we were heading for Rome after all, but I had little idea of time or distance. Then, in a more purposeful fashion, we moved forwards, to the north, and I fell soundly asleep.

When I woke the train was stationary. The headache had vanished and, as often happens, I now felt exuberantly well. Amos was shaking my shoulder, whispering something about taking a look. We scrambled cautiously to our feet and picked our way among bodies to the ventilator. He was tall enough to be able to peer out and reported that we were near a steep bank, that a German sentry was walking up and down the line, and that the night was fairly black.

The train might start again at any minute and there was no time to collect clothes or provisions. He gave me a leg up and I hung for a few seconds half in half out of the ventilator, listening for the sentry's steps. They were moving away. I lowered myself quietly on to the track, scrambled up the bank, and threw myself down in a muddy field that was planted, I vividly remember, with beans. A few seconds later Amos himself lay panting beside me. And after a long minute the train moved off.

As it receded we could hear someone plunging clumsily about in the beans near us. We pressed our faces and bodies in the earth, imagining that we'd been spotted and were being searched for by an Italian peasant or a German soldier. We were being searched for, but by neither.

"Ah, there you are," said the man, joining us.

"Christ, Mark, who asked *you* to come?" I said, but under my breath.

CHAPTER IX

"AND DID THE AMERICANS grab the train and drive it south?" asked Matthew.

"Not that I ever heard."

"You'd have heard all right. There'd have been books galore and an Errol Flynn film."

After a climb to Peter's cave and the Hermitage of Sant' Onofrio, we were picnicking on the terrace of Ovid's villa, in the shade of a wall covered with *opus reticulatum*. Holy Humphrey himself, had he been in residence, could have spat on our heads. We, if we had been cricketers like Amos, could almost have thrown a stone down into the Badia of Santo Spirito, used in this century as a state prison. The sight of armed guards patrolling the high walls quickened memories of my own former prison, the red roofs of which could be seen half a mile below us, near the Fonte d'Amore, where washing glinted among the ilexes. The barracks appeared derelict.

"Any more *vino* left? It goes rather well with the garlic sausage." The good basic things included a red wine bought in Sulmona market for about sixpence a gallon. In other circumstances it would probably have tasted like raw vinegar but in the heat, with the sour bread, bitter black olives, and the rest, one wanted to go on drinking it for ever.

"As much as you like and try some of this cottage cheese. We used to make it ourselves when we kept a cow, but ours never somehow had this flavor."

"I expect your milk was too pure. Food's far better when it's full of germs. This meal is certainly a great improvement on anything yesterday!"

The day before had been a failure pretty well all through. A thunderstorm struck us during a poor lunch in Pescara—why are Adriatic fish usually so dull? We drove back along the road to Popoli in a slow procession of traffic returning frustrated from the coast, and thence to Sulmona which, on a wet Sunday afternoon, was not at its most romantic. Crossing the Vella by a concrete bridge, we entered past petrol pumps, a football stadium, a hideous new hotel, and a dismal municipal garden. The main street, badly bombed in the war and rebuilt, might have been part of Stevenage. The only café we could find open was crowded with bored soldiers and with young peasants trying to look sophisticated to the sounds of a juke box. Matthew, always sweeping in his dislikes, took against the whole place. Nor did a quick tour of the sights win him over. His architectural taste is uncompromisingly austere. He asks for grandeur and simplicity. I'd made the error of telling him to expect both.

"The history of Sulmona," wrote Lear, "is a tissue of evils—war, famine, plague, and earthquake; and, that it now exists at all, is a matter of wonder." (He admired its resilient splendor but found the inn so uninviting that he preferred to ride for the night to Popoli. Despising our own caution we opted for the new hotel, noisy, expensive, impersonal, offering clean sheets, hot water, and, as we soon discovered, not much else.) Ever since my last visit, about six years after the war, I'd cherished the memory of crumbling church façades, often all that still stood of the original building, of stucco palaces with fine stone doorways and Spanish ironwork balconies— a legacy of Bourbon rule, of cavernous side streets vanishing into space through arches in the city walls. Now I found myself explaining to Matthew that of course it all looked quite different with a stronger contrast of sun and shadow. Inside the churches he merely scowled at the richly robed and bejeweled Madonnas and, with more justice, dubbed the invariable baroque restoration fussy and second rate. The rosaries and religious ornaments made from colored sweets, another local speciality, also left him cold.

I'd kept till last the Piazza Garibaldi, a paved amphitheater the size of Wembley Stadium. Mt. Morrone towers above it to the east, the western end is spanned by the pointed arches of a medieval aqueduct, behind which the ruined pile of S. Francesco della Scarpa provides a superb backdrop. But now Morrone was hidden in rain cloud and a bedraggled fair, in process of erection, filled most of the space, wrecking the scale. Matthew brightened instantly. "Ah, this looks more amusing. Let's go on the dodgems." But the fair, we learnt, would not open till the morrow. We wandered round the closed booths, watching the workmen. *Teatro dei Quadrumani* read a mysterious sign above a drawn curtain, flanked by two crude pictures. One showed a gorilla eating a skeleton, the other a naked blonde wrestling with a python. It was not clear *what* had four hands. Back in the hotel, the water was cold, dinner a greasy disaster, and Matthew's bed, he complained bitterly after testing it, *lumpy*. The spivvish manager, engrossed watching Rome television, did not improve matters by telling him in so many words to lump it.

But Monday went beautifully from the start. We breakfasted on the hotel terrace with a view up the whole valley. The mountains on either side, a balanced composition of varying sizes and shapes, led the eye back and ever back to the extreme distance where fluffy clouds perched on the Sasso's horns. Matthew, admitting with a grin that he'd slept soundly in spite of the lumps, pronounced the coffee excellent by any standard and drank six cups. The air, sparkling with moisture and early sunlight, smelt like champagne and Sulmona, when we went for a stroll, needed no word from me to point its virtues. The public garden now struck us as delightful, the modern buildings in the main street as an excellent compromise between vigor and refinement, and the church façades showed off their grandeur and simplicity to perfection.

Mt. Morrone hung like a shimmering grey curtain above the Piazza Garibaldi, where a market squeezed among the dodgems. Stalls displayed home-made wooden spoons and hayforks, dried fish, bright head-cloths, or the large copper urns, with a waist and two slender ear-shaped handles, that look so charming balanced on the heads of peasant women and do so much to form their graceful carriage. The women themselves, some in the traditional costume of Pettorano, Scanno, and other neighboring villages, were present in force to sell their cheeses, peppers, fruit, eggs, poultry. A ferocious party of gipsy girls, dressed in scarlet, orange, and black, screamed abuse and shook their fists at me when, surreptitiously, I tried to take their photograph.

Matthew, who had observed the encounter from a distance, was delighted. "That's the way to deal with tourists! You know, those girls could have been *bedu* from anywhere in Southern Arabia. This place really has something after all."

Later, the little town of Pratola Peligna, as immemorial as its name, reminded him of rock villages in the Hadhramaut. The Romanesque abbey of San Pelino was also sufficiently austere to win his approval. And to complete his sense of well-being he put me right on the name of a bird that hovered near us outside the abbey and that I referred to as a sparrow-hawk. It was, he corrected me, a kestrel. I am not qualified to argue with Matthew about fauna.

Nor, for that matter, about flora. He makes no claims as a botanist but in the course of his travels he has acquired a working knowledge that, compared to mine, is encyclopædic. On the climb to the Hermitage he identified dozens of plants, giving me their names in Arabic, Somali, Urdu, and even English—I could kick myself for having forgotten them all already. In short, by the time we reached Ovid's villa and settled down to our picnic we were both as happy as *alaudae arvenses*.

"After the Armistice on 8th September, some of the other ranks grabbed weapons and freed the state prisoners in the Badia. Among them they found a British officer who had gone mad. I imagine an Italian prison is pretty ghastly at any time. The thought of the wretched men in there now slightly spoils my appetite."

"It increases mine. Pass the bread. And I bet it's not as uncomfortable as our hotel."

"I dare say you're right. Italians are fundamentally too civilized to take the *idea* of punishment seriously—they abolished the death penalty over a century ago. Actually there's rather an amusing story about this prison. In 1957 the Provincial Government at L'Aquila suddenly withdrew Sulmona's status as a military district. Much of its income came from the Army and feeling ran high. There has always been rivalry between the two cities—Sulmona was a capital long before Frederick the Second had been dreamt of. When the news broke, the Prefect of L'Aquila happened to be paying a courtesy visit to the Bishop here. The crowd barricaded him in the Town Hall and he had to be rescued by armored cars. After a day's fighting about fifty rioters were arrested and shut up in the Badia. The next day the women of Sulmona marched out and released their men. And if they were anything like those who attacked me in the market, no wonder they succeeded!"

"Was Sulmona made a military district again?"

"I believe so. Anyway, there are plenty of soldiers around."

There was another angle to the story that intrigued me. The English press had mentioned the incident at the time. In Florence, from curiosity, I'd looked up the back files of the Italian papers. Sulmona's revolution even knocked the Montesi trial in Venice off the national headlines. Much of the trouble, apparently, was caused by an arrogant *carabiniere* captain who had used tear-gas on the crowd. That really made them wild. One of the papers gave his name as Croce. It's a common enough name in the Abruzzi—Benedetto himself was born at Pescasseroli. Still, if our old friend from Vasco had not died after all, his Fascism might easily have halted his career at the rank of captain and I could well imagine him using tear-gas on a mob of peasants. But the coincidence was so improbable that I kept it to myself and instead got Matthew to talk of his recent travels in Persian Kurdistan, fascinated, as always, by his casual reference to bears and ibex and griffon vultures, to black tents pitched by nomads on mountain tops among gentians.

"By the way, what's that called?" I pointed to a plant creeping through Ovid's mosaic floor. "We have it in the garden and I've used it in a still life occasionally because it combines two rather unusual tones of green."

"Spurge. How you have the face to live in the country defeats me. You'd be more at home in Bloomsbury or Chelsea."

"A painter's job is to look, not to remember the names—though God knows I wish I could remember them. My mind seems to be too cluttered up with trivial scraps of conversation to digest any serious knowledge. For instance, I can remember your saying in our first year at Oxford—we were sitting up late in Luke's rooms—that, although you were right-handed, you always used your left to brush your teeth and comb your hair!"

"How odd. I still do. But I haven't the faintest recollection of ever sitting with you in Luke's rooms." Matthew yawned and stretched out contentedly. "*What* a good lunch! And what a marvelously peaceful view. Your Abruzzi remind me a bit of Crete. Or of parts of the Karakorum. Why do people bother with twentieth-century civilization and all its pointless possessions? The simple life for me . . ."

I laughed. "I remember Amos saying exactly the same once, when we were down there."

"He must have been a delightful man. I wish I'd known him better. He was killed, wasn't he, when you got through the lines in the end?"

"Yes. The body was never found. There were minefields, German outposts, the River Sangro was in spate . . . It could have happened in a dozen ways and no one been the wiser. I always thought of him as being rather old. Now I realize he was still under forty— a mere boy."

"Perhaps it was the best solution. I don't think he would have fitted into the post-war world. I feel the same about my brother Luke."

"One says that—to make their deaths more acceptable. Luke, I'm sure, would have become a success as something—a writer, perhaps. Amos, as he often regretted, had no talent, except for piling up debts. But he had wit. He'd have adapted himself easily enough. And how I would have enjoyed watching him . . ."

Matthew embarked on the horrors of the post-war world, lamenting, in a familiar strain, that we've lost our values and are doomed inexorably to destruction. Beside his Cassandra-complex, my own brand of creative pessimism pales to a sterile hopefulness.

"My dear Matthew, I can remember your foretelling the end of civilization in 1932, and every year thereafter till 1939. Soon after we'd both been demobilized, in the autumn of 1945, I lunched with you at the Travellers'. We discussed an article written by a general— I forget which one—that had caused rather a stir. Do you recall the conversation?"

"Not a clue. What did I say?"

"This chap was quite *certain* there wouldn't be a war against Russia for five years. He was *almost* certain there wouldn't be one within ten. But he bet his bottom dollar there *would* be one within fifteen. You thought he'd made a courageous prediction. I thought he'd made a bloody fool of himself."

Matthew sat up a little. "Yes, now you've reminded me, I do recall the conversation. And, what's more, I remember something *you* said—because it haunted me for a while. I was just off on my first trip to the Pamirs and I asked you what you were intending to do with life, now that you had the chance to get on with it. You said something of this sort: 'I don't pray as a rule, but I pray for twenty years of peace. Just twenty years. None of the things I want to do can be done well in less, except by a genius. And if I don't manage to do them in that time, I never shall.'" Matthew looked at me with amusement. "Remember?"

"Only too clearly. It wasn't exactly a prayer. More a sort of bargain between myself and—what you will. Providence, God, perhaps the Devil. The twenty years are nearly up."

"Well? And have you done all you hoped?"

"You know the answer as well as I do. Does anyone do *all* he hoped? Or even a tiny fraction? But I've had twenty wonderful years. I've no right to ask for *another* twenty. If Holy Humphrey drops a boulder on my head before we leave here, you may call the bargain happily settled."

"I shall do nothing of the kind. I'm not in the least superstitious and I don't believe in Providence or whatever. I shall blame that silly old priest who showed us round for criminal carelessness and have him slung into the Badia with the rest. Not because of *you*. But because the boulder might have landed on *me*! You make things too difficult for yourself. Life's quite a simple affair really, or should be. Pass the *vino*."

"Ah, there's enough for one more glass," he said, filling his own. "I expect you wanted it yourself, but the whole of civilization depends . . ."

"The simple life is a daydream, a delusion," I said. "It never has existed and it can't. Because life is governed by people and human relationships are immensely subtle and complicated. From what I hear the nervous tensions in a primitive tribe are just as fierce as in Belgrave Square—and with more drastic results."

But Matthew, as sensitive to human relationships as anyone I know, maintained that the formal pattern of social existence is more important. "In any tribe I've met, everyone has his place and is fundamentally happier as a result. Why, in England nowadays, no one is even sure any longer how to address a stranger properly. Supposing you met Randolph Churchill for the first time at a party and needed to write to him the next day for some reason. Would you start your letter 'Dear Mr. Churchill,' 'Dear Randolph,' 'Dear Churchill,' 'Dear Randolph Churchill,' or what?"

"I'd send a postcard." I drained my own glass, adding, "Anyway, the simple life is too expensive—it costs at least a hundred quid."

"Rubbish. When I'm with the Masai I don't spend a shilling in weeks."

"And how much does your plane ticket cost?"

In a pusillanimous age it is refreshing to have one friend whose convictions are unshakably held. Some of Matthew's strength is due to his ability, when confronted with an unanswerable flaw in his philosophy, to drop off instantly into sleep. He was asleep now.

I leant dreamily back against the *opus reticulatum*, losing myself in a chain of "if" speculations. If Matthew hadn't planned a raid on Sardinia . . . If we hadn't been captured, or if we had been sent to a camp in the north . . . If Amos and I hadn't jumped off the train . . . If, even, Mark hadn't come after us . . . How much would have changed? I wondered. Lucinda and I might have settled somewhere in the English country, we might have had as many children. But certainly I would not have been inspired by the same crazy idea of combining creative art with the self-sufficiency of Italian peasant life. I'd failed in the role of peasant, as in all the rest. And now, twenty years later, here I was back where I'd started. Would there be another twenty years, to try again?

In the afternoon haze, that may have been partly alcoholic, Sulmona looked no more than a jagged outcrop of grey rocks between the Gizio and Vella. Beyond it rose the violet mass of Monte Genzana. I tried to identify the tiny village of Intradacqua in a fold on its northern flank, to locate the position of one or two lower caves, to trace the path that led up diagonally to the highest cave among the beeches that were hidden behind a shoulder. But all the landmarks from this direction were unfamiliar, indeed the whole scene shimmered in a misty unreality, so that I had almost to pinch myself to believe in its existence, or my own.

This valley . . . Really I knew nothing about it or its people. I'd only touched both for a short time in quite out of the ordinary circumstances. I couldn't even speak their language adequately. And yet I was thinking of writing a book about them, a delayed tribute which nevertheless amounted to staking some sort of claim as an authority. What, when one got down to it, could I say? Perhaps only that the chance that had led me to the valley originally, even my presence there again now with Matthew, seemed part of some reassuring if nebulous pattern, a pattern that would vanish if I attempted to define it too clearly.

The train from Roccaraso rattled over the viaducts on Monte Rotella, to be met, a quarter of an hour later, by its cousin descending from Cocullo. A lorry backfired on the road from Popoli. Nearer, somewhere, the stutter of a motorbike obtruded above the cicadas' hum. Otherwise there was little evidence of the present century. In its essentials life in the valley had barely changed for 2000 years. But it had never been *simple* . . .

And certainly not around midnight of 30th September, 1943, I thought, before I too fell asleep.

Two's company, they say . . . For general purposes I have usually found three a more amusing combination. Before long Amos and I were glad enough to have Mark with us, but at first his unexpected presence filled us merely with alarm. We had both had a good deal of experience of creeping about in unknown enemy countryside, whereas his ineptitude, indeed distaste, for playing Red Indians had been demonstrated at Athlit. In any case a third person would make stealth or a snap decision far more difficult. However, whether we liked it or not, there he now was breathing noisily in the beans beside us.

"We managed that rather well, I thought," he panted. (Some years ago he published a charming and erudite volume of autobiography.[1] In it, where he briefly mentions his escape, he refers to "two other officers who had followed me out of the truck." The most meticulous of scholars, he may be grateful to have the record put straight.)

Where the devil were we? A mile or two to the south we made out the subdued lights of a town which, if the train had traveled that

[1] *Remote and ineffectual Don* by Mark Duffy. Oxbridge Press 25s.

far, might be Popoli, but which, discussing it, we concluded was still
Sulmona. We could identify the mass of Morrone to the east and
various other landmarks. Further mountains loomed to the south-
west, in the direction of Naples. The clear sky behind the range was
continually lit by flashes that we hoped were signs of a battle but
that were only summer lightning. Still, if we could only manage to
cross the range we might reach the Allied line in a week or less.

Between us we had two bread rolls, a packet of raisins, and a tin
of Canadian potted meat. For literature we had *The Bridge of San
Luis Rey* which I happened to be carrying in my pocket. We were
dressed in khaki drill trousers and bush shirts. I wore the rubber-
soled boots that I'd used for parachuting into Sardinia, the others
gym shoes. Mark contributed no food but, of more value, a heavy
greatcoat in which he had somehow squeezed through the ventilator, and, of more value still, a small map of Italy torn out of a
guide-book in the prison library. With luck we should find fruit and
vegetables before reaching the mountains. After that, who could
tell? There was always Palestine soup.

We set off through the fields with extreme caution, jumping out
of our skins at every shadow, then gaining confidence. We passed the
occasional farmstead where the dogs barked, but otherwise heard no
one—and found nothing more to eat than a raw marrow which we
carried with us. Mark's shortcomings as a companion soon showed
themselves. Though lightly built he was incorrigibly clumsy, stum-
bling and crashing through a crop of unripe maize like a bull ele-
phant. He was also rather deaf and seemed unable to lower the pitch
of his voice. If we hissed "For God's sake, *quiet!*" he was liable to
shout "*What* did you say?" Lastly he was greedy, constantly lagging
behind in a quest for food. At one point we lost him altogether and
spent ten precious minutes retracing our steps. "I'm damned if I'll
go on with this three-legged race much farther," Amos growled.
"Tell your friend that if he doesn't keep up he can travel alone."

"*My* friend!"

We came on him at length in a vineyard. The grapes had all
been harvested but nevertheless he was hunting round in case any
remained.

We were still in the cultivation when dawn glimmered. As a
hide-up a bamboo clump beside a stream was far from ideal, but

the best that offered. Crawling into the center we thickened it round us with broken stems and leaves and huddled together on the damp earth with the greatcoat over us. After half an hour the cold became almost unbearable and it was impossible to lie absolutely still. The spine, least protected by flesh, is the part of the body that feels the cold worst. Then and thereafter we discovered that the best way to keep warm was for two to lie back to back, while the third lay with his back against the front of one of the others. We also learnt that, provided you have a small hollow for your hip bone to fit into, you can sleep quite comfortably even on rock.

In the Gizio Valley, as in any cultivated part of Italy, an unfrequented spot hardly exists. Every inch of soil, however barren, is visited daily by some old man or woman whose very life depends on it. At night our bamboo clump had looked an unlikely place for anyone to come to, but soon after dawn a peasant and his small son arrived with a ladder and a long pole, in order to shake the nuts off an adjacent walnut tree. The nuts fell in an arc of which the closest point was barely five yards from us. The man and boy were joined by their women and all spent hours crawling round the arc on hands and knees. They never spotted us but the suspense was nerve-racking. Throughout the day other peasants passed by us along the bank of the stream and, to stretch our nerves further, the stream made the sound of approaching footsteps. Mark dozed off and began to snore. "Anything the matter?" he exclaimed irritably when we woke him.

Evening came at last, the landscape emptied and, breathing more freely, we gnawed as much as we could stomach of the marrow. We had already finished the bread and raisins but were keeping the tin of meat in reserve. After dark we started again towards the mountains, crossing the railway line that leads from Sulmona to Cocullo. The ground rose gradually through vineyards where the grapes had not yet been picked. We munched them as we went, stuffing our pockets with more. The cultivation ended abruptly, the mountain began. For a couple of hours we scrambled up through a rocky wood, determined to get well clear of the valley, and at dawn found ourselves in a stretch of sparse oak scrub. We settled down under a small bush rather than venture on to an open expanse above.

"Well, so far so good," said Amos.

"Better than our last attempt, anyway," I said. "I suppose the rest of them are half-way to Germany by now."

As the light increased Sulmona peeped round the mountain's shoulder and we could see the station. "Poor old Kempster," said Amos. "I'm afraid I was always rather bloody to him."

"Do you mean the man who was shot?" asked Mark, "I didn't know he was a friend of yours. I thought he was a Yugoslav."

"He was half-German," I explained. "He'd joined up with the Yugoslavs—I think to avoid being identified. Very brave of him to make a dash but it was a dotty place to try. But you knew Kempster, surely. He was at Athlit."

"Of course. I'd forgotten. Anyway, two chaps who saw it happen were discussing it in the train. According to them he wasn't trying to escape at all. He was standing a yard or two away from the rest and a sentry suddenly shot him. I suppose it's possible the Germans had found out about him—there were spies everywhere in that camp."

"Are either of you *certain* he was the man who was shot?" asked Amos.

"I saw nothing," said Mark, "except a pair of hobnailed boots sticking out under a sack."

"Well, I didn't examine the corpse," I said. "But the description tallied exactly. And none of the other Yugoslavs was wearing a *shech*, or anything like one, round his neck. I'm afraid it was certainly him. Hadn't we all better try to sleep?"

None of us had slept for more than an hour or two in the past forty-eight and we failed to do so now. The ground was steep and pebbly, a bitter wind chilled us to the marrow, and we were damnably hungry. Then it started to rain. A light drizzle that became a steady downpour. The bush gave no protection, the greatcoat little more. Rivulets trickled down the pebbles under us and present misery soon outweighed any sense of jubilation at our precarious freedom.

Mountains are always so much larger than you expect. "They're steep and wild as hell. You'd die of exposure in a day or two, if you hadn't died of thirst or starved to death first." At the time I'd thought Polly's pessimism exaggerated. Now it struck me as only too accurate. There must be watering points for the sheep on the high pastures, if we could locate them, but there was precious little chance of finding food, except with the shepherds. And they, we had to assume, would hand us over at once.

We were out of the bag for the moment; but still a long way from safety. I was fitter than the other two, perhaps more determined to reach home, but I knew I couldn't last more than another day or so of hard climbing, let alone a week, without something solid to eat. And what happened if we developed malaria? Amos and I, alone of the Sardinian party, had so far escaped it but the infection often took weeks to appear. Evidently he was thinking on the same lines. "It must be about eleven-thirty. Only another six hours of this before we can stretch our legs. And I can't say I trust mine to carry me very far."

A grey mist had closed right in. We hung suspended above the invisible Gizio Valley in a cotton-woolly limbo, lost souls with small prospect, that any of us could imagine, of salvation. It was at that point that Mark revealed his worth as a companion. He talked.

Amos and I were never exactly at a loss for words. Sharing many tastes and friends and past experiences, we could always gossip to while away the time if we felt like it. But we'd heard one another's ideas and opinions so often that they no longer stimulated. Left to ourselves we tended to be taciturn, like a devoted husband and wife. Mark, the odd-man-out, was an invaluable catalyst, someone to be beastly about when he wasn't with us, who always had something provocative or amusing to say when he was. In his own common room, where competition is doubtless stiffer, he is not reckoned much of a conversationalist, I believe. His colleagues see the morose don we had met at Athlit. But now, and in the following weeks, when talk was often the sole means of taking our minds off our empty stomachs, the cold, a growing state of anxiety, or whatever, we came to know a more sociable side to him. Admittedly he enjoyed the sound of his own voice—enjoyed it occasionally more than we did. He could be immensely irritating. But irritation is a wonderful calorific and not the least contribution that Mark often made was to keep us warm.

Of course I've long since forgotten the gist of our innumerable conversations but I do partly recall the first, chiefly because it was

such an odd one to have, lying on a strange mountain in the rain
and in desperate circumstances. He talked about Ovid.

"It's tragic, don't you think, the way generations of schoolmas-
ters have used him to torture their pupils. The *Metamorphoses*, for
instance. Much too difficult for schoolboys. Why not give them the
Ars Amatoria? They'd learn Latin quickly enough then! I mean, old
Naso was essentially so jolly, so *human*, don't you agree?" Mark had
a pleasantly ironical way of pretending we were as well-educated as
himself. "Really it's all wrong to concentrate wholly on the academic
content of a poet for academic purposes. To castrate him, so to
speak, before serving him up. Not—as you will rightly point out—
that scholarship is not important in poetry. Indeed it is. Ovid—
since we're discussing him—was the repository of the knowledge
of his age. The trouble with our contemporaries is that they don't
know enough. They have no *weight*. They can only describe *feelings*,
the surge of the blood and all that. Their poems are sensitive little scraps of emotion—the sort of thing the great poets of the past
simply threw in for good measure. Pound, you may say, has tried
to restore scholarship to poetry but I always suspect that all those
obscure quotations, all those scraps of Chinese and Italian and so
on, are put in more for effect than because they mean anything.
Don't you agree?"

"Agree with what?" said Amos, crossly. He lay between us, protruding from either end of the greatcoat. His eyes were closed and
two days' worth of stubble on his chin gave his face the pallor of
a corpse. Rain glistened on his hair and eyelashes and he looked
worn out.

"That he's really showing off a bit."

"Who is?"

"Pound. We've been discussing him."

"Damn Pound. Let's discuss this problem. If we open the tin of
meat it may give us enough strength to climb farther up this mountain, but then we'll have nothing left and we can't be sure of finding
anything. On the other hand, if we save the tin, we may not have
the strength to climb more than another hundred feet."

"I'm in favor of eating it," I said. "Once we get higher up, out
of sight of the valley, it will be safer to search around for food in

daylight. There are bound to be roots and berries and that sort of thing."

"Oh, no. None of your Palestine soup again," said Mark. "Let old Ovid have the last word on the subject, though actually he was talking about painting the face. I came on it in the library. *'Nec vos graminibus nec mixto credite socco . . .'* Which, to remind you, means, 'Don't trust to grasses, nor to a mixture of juices.' I don't intend to trust them. I'd sooner starve."

The conversation irritated Amos. It impressed me. I was exactly thirty years and one day old, and I was many kinds of a snob, but an intellectual snob foremost. How splendid to be able to quote Ovid. To be able to quote anything, come to that.

Amos's irritation exploded. "For Christ's sake stop being so clever-clever. We've got a bloody great mountain ahead of us and no *food*. You've helped to eat the food we brought. What's *your* contribution?"

"The greatcoat. It's covering more of you than me, but I'll go and lie under another bush if that will satisfy you."

The quarrel between them flared for a few more exchanges, then died down. They laughed, as they usually managed to laugh, eventually. We agreed to open the tin of meat before starting at nightfall. The rain came down still harder. Mark told us about Petrarch, comparing him with D. H. Lawrence—to the latter's disadvantage, if I remember correctly. After a while we gave up reminding him to talk less loudly. About four-thirty a dog appeared suddenly out of the mist, sniffed at us, and barked. Footsteps crunched on the pebbles and a few seconds later we were surrounded by a group of wild young men armed to the teeth.

The souls were to be delivered from limbo. But to where? The delivering angels waved their revolvers and there was a moment's doubt which side they represented.

"Oh, God. Not into the bag again!" said Amos.

"Inglesi," said Mark. *"Siamo inglesi!"*

Then the angels shook us by the hand. "The Germans are all running away!" they shouted. "The Allied army will arrive in Sulmona tomorrow. Or the day after . . ."

CHAPTER X

MONTE GENZANA, as it will be convenient to call the whole range
south-west of Sulmona though there are several other peaks, reaches
6500 feet, a few hundred feet higher than Monte Rotella that faces
it across the upper Gizio Valley, and about one thousand five hundred feet less than the Maiella which sweeps majestically across the
horizon to the north-east, a gigantic sow's back as the name implies.
At that time the wooded lower slopes of Genzana sheltered scores
of *giovanotti* hiding up there by day to escape being impressed for
labor and sent to Germany. Many carried some kind of weapon
which they loved to fire off into the air to show that it worked. They
boasted, and perhaps believed, that the Germans did not dare to
come up after them.

At night most of the *giovanotti* returned to their homes. Our lot,
about ten in number, had taken over a small stone hut where, in the
best Abruzzese tradition, they played at being brigands, requisitioning food from the nearest farms. The hut lay hidden in a re-entrant
a mile above the village of Intradacqua, out of sight of Sulmona and
looking north to the Sasso. They led us down there through the
mist, made space for us on the straw-covered floor, fed us steaming bowls of bean soup, and, to our inexpressible relief, treated us as
honored guests.

"Tomorrow, when your friends arrive, it will be your turn to do the same for us," they cried, when we tried to thank them. "Tomorrow. The day after at the latest."

With them in the hut we found four British soldiers, escaped P.O.W.s in civilian clothes, who told us they had been walking for two weeks down the valleys from L'Aquila and had everywhere met with kindness and help from the peasants. As on various similar occasions in the future, I was struck by how naturally the soldiers accepted peasant hospitality. Uninhibited by language difficulties, they shared with the *giovanotti* a spontaneous human warmth which we consciously lacked. Their "Give us some more of that soup, cock. It's bloody good" was better understood, and appreciated, than our refined "Well, if you're *sure* you can spare it" sort of politeness. "Eat up, man," one of them said to me, noticing my hesitation at taking a second portion. "These peasants have tons of scoff tucked away. It's all they live for. Why not help them finish it? Look at the thousands there are of them in England, finishing *our* food—and probably raping my wife and yours into the bargain. So eat up!"

The *giovanotti* produced a flask of *vino* and by candlelight we all celebrated our imminent liberation, before sleeping for a dozen blissful hours tightly wedged together in the straw. Next morning the soldiers set off to continue south by the valleys, enviably confident that they'd get through the lines eventually without much trouble. We exchanged names, to be able to pass on news of one another. Theirs I wrote on Kempster's scrap of paper, ours on a fly-leaf torn from *The Bridge of San Luis Rey*. I was about to add the name and address of Kempster's sister, asking them to report his death, but Mark sensibly advised against it. If they were caught it might get them, or her, into trouble. "What a small world," he added, reading the address. "The Piazza San Martino di Parma. A charming little backwater near the Boboli Gardens. I once stayed with friends who had a house there. If I'm ever in Florence after the war I'll try to contact her."

The question was whether to follow the soldiers' example and walk boldly south, or remain where we were. Amos and I wanted to walk, but across the mountains. Remembering Joe's experience, we were unwilling to trust the generosity of peasants in spite of what the soldiers said. Mark was ready to trust the peasants but refused to climb mountains. He pointed out that neither he nor Amos had proper shoes and that we'd soon find ourselves without food again. "We'll feel bloody fools if we've starved to death up there when the Eighth Army drives into Sulmona." "Still bloodier fools," we said, "if we've let ourselves be caught here when we could so easily have waited in safety." The argument grew heated. "The whole of civilization depends on someone being prepared to give way," said Mark. "As you've mentioned before," said Amos. "I notice that it's never *you* who does the giving."

In the end we did the giving—and agreed that, if the *giovanotti* would keep us, we were probably best off with them for the time being. They were a rough and ready crowd, enjoying themselves in much the same sort of way that we had at Athlit, except that they saw themselves as a reckless band of brigands dominating the neighborhood. We had to listen to interminable accounts of their exploits, and of one in particular which their volubility and our weak Italian prevented us from ever quite grasping. The day before our arrival, apparently, they had raided Intradacqua, beaten up the *carabiniere* sergeant who was a noted Fascist, and threatened him with more unless he helped them to get all the supplies they needed. Amos and I had no love for *carabinieri*, having ourselves been beaten up by them in Sardinia, but we began to feel sorry for this one if all the things the *giovanotti* said they had done to him were true. The story cheered us for a different reason. The Fascist Government was back in power. We knew that the *giovanotti* would not dare even to boast of the deed unless they were confident that the Allies would reach the valley almost immediately.

After three days there were still no signs of an approaching battle. "Your army will arrive the day after tomorrow. Next week for certain," they assured us, but with less conviction. They begged us to keep out of sight in the hut, in case rumors of our presence spread abroad—the nearest cultivation was only a few hundred yards away. Understandably their hospitality had begun to wane, the charm of their company also. But we stayed on, in conditions of considerable squalor and in an atmosphere of growing tension.

The main trouble, of course, was Mark.

Amos, with aristocratic adaptability, rubbed along with them well enough, amused by their exuberant chatter and indifferent to the dirt, while my *nostalgie de la boue* made the pigsty life in the hut positively congenial. But Mark had more fastidious standards. Not to be able to comb his hair or to wash caused him acute discomfort of mind as well as of body. When handed a bowl of macaroni he would look instinctively for a spoon whereas we, though no hungrier, gobbled it happily with our fingers. Our companions and their crude habits disgusted and enraged him. And having lived most of his life in the academic world he was not used to hiding his antipathies.

"They're really not as bad as all that," we remonstrated. "For heaven's sake try to be more civil. You're putting their backs up—and we're utterly dependent on them!"

The leader of the gang was admittedly odious by any reckoning. Large, fat, and swarthy, he seemed as full of wind as a bagpipe and his incessant boasting, and still louder belching, grated on us all. Mark called him simply The Hog, "a specimen of that kind of disposition and temper (to quote, once more, the inimitably ponderous Keppel Craven on an encounter with The Hog's great-grandfather) which, without justifying absolute ill-usage or violence, is formed of such irritating materials as to render the necessity of such painful measures a matter of ever-recurring speculation."

The antagonism between Mark and The Hog was mutual and had more than a personal basis. It was a clash between a brash descendant of the bronze-age Peligni and a scarcely less thick-skinned representative of unyielding Oxford superiority. Fortunately The Hog spent most of the day up in the woods firing off his revolver.

But these were minor vexations and we were more grateful for our good fortune than it sounds. Given adequate food and warmth, comfort depends in the end on a few very small things. Tangled hair and beard, a begrimed face, hands and body, are soon accepted as the natural state, but a minute thorn in the foot can make one pray for a needle or pair of fine tweezers. Perhaps the essential requirements may be reduced to a tooth-brush and a nail-file—we cleaned our teeth with the green twigs of an apricot tree and rubbed down our finger and toenails with sandstone. To which I would add a third, that Logan Pearsall Smith somewhere indicates. "Amid the vast unimportance of all things, how beyond all calculation important we find it each morning to have at hand, as we sit facing Time and Eternity, an adequate supply of thin paper!" We wished *The Bridge of San Luis Rey* had been ten times as long.

There were no Germans nearer than Sulmona. Boredom soon became, as it long remained, the most pressing enemy. We sat in the sun on the step of the hut memorizing poetry, of which Mark carried an almost inexhaustible supply around in his head. He had profited, even more than I had, from his sojourn at Vasco and could tell us a good deal about the Abruzzi's history. He talked not only of Ovid and Peter of Morrone, but of dozens of strange figures connected with the valley—of saints and ecclesiastics such as Thomas of Celano, the friend and biographer of St. Francis, or Rienzi, who had also lived for a time at the Badia of Santo Spirito; of brigands like the semi-mythical Marco Sciarra, who, according to the legend, held up Torquato Tasso and then, learning who the poet was, let him pass with a flourish of compliments. He talked, too, of the measures taken against the brigands in the last century, first by the French General Manhes, then later by the famous *carabiniere* Chiaffredo Bergia, a sort of Wyatt Earp figure, who cleaned up Scanno, Pettorano, and other villages on Genzana and finished brigandage in the Abruzzi once and for all by 1870.

In one respect only was Mark a cultural disappointment. He might be able to read Dante, but he was useless at making himself understood in the local dialect. Moreover his innate reserve and perfectionism handicapped him from indulging in the sort of gibberish which Amos and I talked happily with the *giovanotti*, to whom Mark's carefully articulated classical Italian might have been ancient Greek. You can get a long way with goodwill and gestures; still further with iconography. Once when Mark, with rising annoyance, had failed to explain his meaning, I expressed it for him with instant success by merely drawing a fork in the dust.

By the end of a week something obviously had to be done. We couldn't go on hiding in the hut, expecting the *giovanotti* to feed us and with no news beyond their excited rumors. "We should have walked to start with and no nonsense," said Amos, digging at Mark. "We'd have been safely back in England by now."

"Or in the bag," said Mark. "Why fuss? They haven't pushed us out yet, though I thought the soup last night was below par.

And you'll be pleased to hear that I had quite an affable chat with The Hog this morning. I told him that the original inhabitants of this valley must have been exactly like him and I could see he was pleased. Primitive people are always so ancestor-proud. Whereas I'm not in the least ashamed that I'm not the tenth transmitter of a foolish face and that my grandfather sold whelks in Belfast."

"But you *are* ashamed. That's why you keep telling us about him . . ."

That evening The Hog agreed to take me into Intradacqua, to listen to the wireless in the house of some peasants he knew. Amos was too conspicuous, Mark *persona non grata*. The *giovanotti* rigged me up with a hat, coat, and trousers and at dusk The Hog and I slipped down through vineyards and olives to the outskirts of the village, a honeycomb of stone-tiled roofs and cobbled alleys. We waited till dark before entering the single narrow street and from bravado strolled down it as far as a venerable church and back, among a crowd of elderly men. The street was lit only by a few subdued lights coming through doorways where the women, in black shawls, sat knitting. I tried to look like the rest of them, as if I, too, had spent my life gathering timber from the mountain, pruning vines and olives, or ploughing the red earth, but of course they knew perfectly well who I was, and probably had known all about the three of us from the moment we joined the *giovanotti*.

Bravado still getting the better of discretion, The Hog stood me a *grappa* in the pub while he gossiped to some friends. "An Italian from the north, from Milan," I understood him to say, indicating me. "He's feeling sad—just lost his wife." The peasants nodded politely without noticeable disbelief or curiosity when I ventured a *buona sera* with a strong Milanese accent.

Another customer, leaning by the door, called back some word like "*carabiniere.*" The Hog grabbed my arm and we left abruptly, vanishing into the honeycomb through a labyrinth of passages and steps on the steep hillside. At length he tapped a shutter; a door creaked open enough to let us in and was quietly closed again. We entered a large kitchen, dark save for the embers of a fire and the small glow of wireless valves in a corner. Oscillations and a babble of different languages came over the air, as knobs were twiddled in search of the B.B.C. We got it, too. And I caught the end of a pep-talk in French to the Belgians on the subject of Germany's low morale. "*Courage, citoyens Belges . . . et bonne nuit,*" said the announcer, closing down. The radio was switched off and hidden under a sack of grain.

"Is the English news good?" asked several eager voices in the murky smoke-filled room.

As best I could in my Italian I replied, "Very good. The Army will be here next week—probably."

Someone lit a candle, revealing a large family who ranged from an old grandmother to a new-born baby, the mother suckling it by the fire. They were delightful people, even their *giovanotti* appearing more civilized in the home circle, and they insisted on my eating a plate of polenta. The Hog wanted to get back but the grandfather, a wizened old man called Paolo, had lived before the First War in the States and did not intend to miss the chance of showing off his few words.

"You O.K., fella. Me O.K. Them Germans, they not O.K."

"Them not O.K. at all. You're dead right."

"Right. That's it. Them guys sons of bitches."

"You've hit the nail on the head, Paolo."

"Yes, your army hit them. They all run away from Sulmona. All of them."

"Run away? Are you sure?"

"Sure, they run. Trucks, many trucks. Take them sons of bitches Germany. Ha ha."

We kept up a jolly conversation on these lines for some minutes, Paolo shaking my hand warmly every so often while his family nodded admiringly at his possession of that only passport to prosperity, the English language. Other peasants crept quietly in from the night, having got wind of my presence and anxious to share in this portent of delivery.

The Hog, increasingly restive at the publicity, tried again to leave, but the leader of the reckless band of brigands cut little ice in this household. "Him not O.K.," said Paolo. "Him silly ass—my grandson. I no speak English. Forget all, all. Come with me other house. Man there, he speak well. Also priest. Plenty wine. Ha ha."

The Hog protesting, we were led to a house farther up the alley, into a room with more pretentious furniture and mezzotints of reli-

gious subjects. A paraffin lamp gave a good light. The priest in
person handed out glasses of *vino santo* while the man who spoke
English well was being fetched from a bedroom above. I could hear
his footsteps on the stair. And in walked *il professore*.

The pleased astonishment when he recognized me was tempered
for a second by another expression which I interpreted as suspicion,
or perhaps guilt. I wondered if he felt he had abandoned us at Vasco,
but I was much too glad to see him to care what had happened at
the camp. Here at last was someone reliable who would have proper
news and who could advise us what to do next.

"You escaped from Vasco?"

"No, off the train, with two friends. We're living up in the woods
with this young man."

"Are they feeding you well?"

"Very well. But . . ."

He patted The Hog on the shoulder, telling him to keep the
good work up. But The Hog looked merely browned off.

Il professore quickly gave his news. After the Armistice he had
had to visit relatives in Sulmona—or he would have been to see us.
With the return to power of the Fascists things had become trickier for him. His contacts with the British were well known and he'd
had to hide with the priest who was a cousin. He had been listening
regularly to the B.B.C. According to the latest news the Allies were
at Naples on one coast, at Termoli on the other, and nearing Isernia
in the center—about sixty miles from Sulmona. "They should be
here in ten days or a fortnight."

"Would you advise us to walk towards them or wait?"

"Wait, certainly. For the present, at least. Most of the peasants
will help you, but not all. There are many other escaped prisoners in
the valley, and little food." He rubbed his chin thoughtfully. "But if
your army does not come in a month, I don't think it will before the
spring. The weather alone could prevent the advance." He smiled,
apologetically. "I would offer to help you myself but tomorrow I am
returning to Vasco, to my school. Term has started and I've had a
message that there will be no danger if I go back now. They need
teachers! I advise you to wait till the end of October. Then, if your
army still hasn't arrived, walk as fast as you can—after that there

will be snow. The mountains are terribly hard unless you know them. You wouldn't get across without a guide. Much depends on yourselves. Who are the others with you?"

He hadn't heard of Amos but made a face when I mentioned Mark. "*Tenente* Duffy . . . You did not choose your companion well."

"I didn't choose him at all. But he's all right. Why don't you like him?"

"He's a—what's the word? a busybody, a double-crosser. He asks others to do the work and run the risks, so he can take the credit." He spoke with sudden anger.

"Well, I know what you mean, in a way . . ." I said, amused.

"He also owes me much money. I am a poor man. Perhaps I was foolish to buy what he asked."

"Do you mean you bought things for the camp? Food and so on?"

"Not food. Three pairs of boots, a rope, electric wire, a spade, a hammer, nails. Such things. They were not so expensive. But something else cost a lot, more than three thousand lire. I had myself to borrow the money to pay for it. That was one reason why I had to leave Vasco."

This was fascinating. "What was it you bought?"

"Explosive. Thirty kilos, altogether. *Tenente* Duffy said it was for weapons, grenades I think. He told me there would be a parachute landing at Vasco or Pescara. The officers in the camp would break out and fight the Germans, if they could make grenades."

"I see." In Mark's defence I explained, "Of course he could hardly have given you cash at the time. I suppose he intended you to be paid—later. It did seem possible there would be a landing."

Il professore laughed rather bitterly. "Well, there wasn't. I don't criticize the *tenente* for that. But I criticize him for telling Croce— what I'd done."

"He told Croce! Oh, surely not? Why should he?"

"I don't know *why*. That, some day perhaps, I shall find out. But I am sure he did tell him. Croce admitted it—I went to see him in hospital, the night of the Armistice. He was very ill, and afraid then what would happen to him if the British army came. It caused me much trouble afterwards—when the army did not come."

"Anyway Croce's dead now, I hear."

"No, he's not dead, but still very ill. They have moved him to a hospital in Rome. And I hope your troops arrive before he recovers! Because he blames *me* for the loss of his arm . . . But I can see that your young man is impatient to leave. He's right. There are too many gossips in Intradacqua."

We parted with a promise to celebrate in Sulmona on Liberation Day. "Please don't mention what I have said to *Tenente* Duffy. But, if I was you, I would bear it in mind." *Il professore* had a remarkable grasp of the finer shades of colloquial English.

"You sound as if you've had the whale of a time," said Amos, when I had rejoined them in the hut. "But has it got us any farther?"

"Well, it's useful to know that the Belgians now have a low opinion of German morale. And old Paolo promised to help us if the *giovanotti* don't."

"How odd that you ran into that little schoolmaster," said Mark. "I never trusted him myself. I believe he double-crossed us with Croce, but the Armistice came before I could prove it. I suppose you hadn't time to talk about Vasco?"

"Not really. By the way he sent greetings to you."

In the interest of Fraternity, Amos and I had agreed to keep off the whole subject of Mark's part in the Vasco debacle and I thought it politic to say nothing of what *il professore* had told me. But I bore it in mind.

We were all woken early the next morning by Paolo himself in a state of breathless excitement. An advance party of Germans had driven into Intradacqua at dawn, to arrange billets for a further hundred troops who would arrive during the day. When they heard the news the *giovanotti* skeltered off without even wishing us goodbye.

"Them fellows not O.K.," said Paolo grimly. He told us to remain quietly in the hut till nightfall, when he would return to guide us to some friends of his in a hamlet two miles away. We thankfully accepted, without asking *why* he was sure his friends would have us, or *how* they had already heard of our existence.

There was nothing in the least like an organized Resistance Movement in the Abruzzi. There was no need for one. The peasants themselves were, as they had always been, a Resistance Movement by tradition and instinct. From the moment Paolo took us over—

though we could not know that—we were in the keeping of something for which I can find no name, though this book is an attempt to do so. Call it essential human dignity, or pride, or just goodness, perhaps.

After dark, with Paolo in the lead, we crept in single-file down the hill past Intradacqua and worked our way round the shoulder of Genzana, skirting the highest fringe of cultivation. The smell of manure in unseen cow byres mingled with the scent of mint and thyme from the mountain, as we slipped between lines of poplar and acacia or trod on the soft bank of an irrigation rivulet, bridged in places by stone slabs. Mark stumbled incessantly, of course. "*What* did you say?" he boomed.

After a couple of hours of this Paolo told us to wait for him while he disappeared ahead into the deep shadow of a tree-clump, through which the silhouette of a roof could dimly be discerned. In the distance a clock in Sulmona chimed eleven. Ten minutes later he was back. "O.K., boys," he whispered and we followed him into a farmyard, where another shadowy shape waited. A door was opened for us to pass quietly through. From the sounds, we were in a pig-sty. Someone lit a candle and we got a view of our host, a cheerful youngish peasant called Gabriele. His pretty young wife entered by another door carrying a bottle and glasses. We all toasted one another in home-made brandy. Then Paolo left and Gabriele settled us down in a pile of clean straw. Our neighbors softly grunted.

"Pigs are certainly an improvement on the *giovanotti*!" said Mark, as we fell asleep.

CHAPTER XI

"WHEN ARE WE GOING to meet your famous peasants?" Matthew's question woke me.

"Later this evening. They'll be busy in the fields till dark and I don't want to be more nuisance than I can help. On the way to Sulmona I just want to call in at the barracks—to tie up a few loose ends in my mind. I also want to go to the station—I've never been back there either. Then we'll have a drink on that little piazza with Ovid's statue and visit my friends before dinner. I expect they're too old to climb the mountain with us tomorrow and I believe their sons are all in Venezuela or somewhere, but they may produce a guide. I'd probably lose the way on my own."

"Remember I have to be back in Florence by Wednesday afternoon."

"You'll do it easily. If we start the climb early we'll be down again by two or three. Reach Rome for a late dinner and catch the fast train in the morning. Florence by midday. When's your date?"

"Lord. I've forgotten the time and place. I'd better ring up from the hotel tonight. Let's start. It's getting chilly up here."

We drove down to the Fonte d'Amore and up the bumpy lane to the barracks. Washing festooned the perimeter wire, chickens scratched round the walls and children played football on the old parade ground. A jolly group of men sat drinking wine in the garden of a cottage. One of them called out that he was the custodian, if I wanted him. I explained my reason for wishing to look inside the barracks and he came over.

Surely no other people have such a gift for squeezing the maximum out of any unexpected situation and the custodian, a burly blue-eyed man of forty, worthily upheld the national tradition. Ah, so I had been a prisoner there in the war? What a terrible time that was! German soldiers everywhere. No food. Thousands of *Inglese* and *Americani* hiding in the mountains. He had only been a *giovanotto* but he had helped feed some of them, had guided others up the Maiella. And it had been so dangerous! The Germans had shot many, many. He himself had been wounded by a machine-gun bullet—he pulled up a sleeve to display the scar, laughing happily at the recollection of that heroic period. His friends gathered round, the older men seizing the chance to tell their own terrible experiences, the younger ones listening skeptically, the way younger ones do.

I could have stayed gossiping about their courage and sacrifices for hours. There are few things I enjoy more than the glow of a shared reminiscence. But after twenty minutes Matthew, excluded from the glow, began to grow restive, so I asked again if I could see inside the barracks.

The custodian threw his hands up dramatically. Alas, what a pity, he couldn't oblige me. The huts were an army ammunition store. There was a *carabiniere* captain in charge and perhaps he would have let me look round but today was *festa*. The poor chap— *il povero*—was away in Sulmona.

"The poor chap?"

Yes, he too had been wounded in the war, had lost an arm. There had been other troubles. Now he was on half-pay, with the job of looking after the ammunition store.

"What's the captain's name? In case I come back tomorrow."

"Capitano Croce."

"Has he lost his right arm or his left?"

One or two thought the right, the others the left. They couldn't be sure. They didn't often see him.

The *carabiniere* captain who had caused the riot might well have been taken off active duty and put in charge of an ammunition dump. It was the sort of thing I'd known to happen often enough in my own army days.

"He is a little *pazzo*"—the custodian tapped his head—"and no one can enter without his permission. It would be most unwise to try. The huts are guarded by a savage dog that bites strangers."

"An Alsatian?" I hazarded.

"Well, a sort of Alsatian. A cross between that and an Abruzzi sheep dog. *Molto feroce.*"

"You have Alsatians on the brain," said Matthew. "Come on, let your ghosts lie in peace."

"Won't be long. As we're getting on so well there are just one or two other things I want to ask him, for my book. But I mustn't seem too inquisitive—it may put him off." To the custodian I said, "We've been up to Ovid's villa. I gather it's a temple of Hercules now."

He grinned and winked. "I'm only an ignorant man. The professors are very clever and learned. But they're human like you and me. They often don't know as much as they pretend."

"Exactly. All guess work." We had a good laugh at professors. "Do people believe that Ovid still haunts this part of the countryside?"

A citizen of Glastonbury could not have looked more surprised if you'd asked him whether he saw much of St. Joseph of Arimathea. Ovid haunt the neighborhood? What an idea. Simple peasants like his own grandmother may have believed something of the kind in the past. But all that sort of superstitious nonsense was finished. Sulmona was a *modern* town. Several of the cafés even had television.

Then I broached my last point.

I'd heard, I said casually, that the Sulmonese, a few years ago, had barricaded the Prefect of L'Aquila in the Town Hall . . .

But at the mention of the episode he and the others all started to talk so loudly and so fast that I couldn't make out whether their sympathies were with the rioting peasants or with the Provincial Government. In fact I could hardly follow a word. They kept it up for ten minutes. Then they asked, a trifle aggressively, what *I* thought. I did what in such a predicament in Italy I always do. I made an expressive gesture with my hands and said *"Ma!"* It seemed an acceptable comment but it didn't get me any further in my quest for Croce. Matthew could no longer be contained and since I valued his good humor more than the satisfaction of my idle curiosity we bade the custodian and his friends goodbye.

The station is just north of the town, astride one of the ancient sheep-ways along which, till the present century, flocks of a million head were driven up from the Apulian Plain to the mountain pastures in spring, and back for the winter. I wanted to go there again as an experiment, to see if the visit to the site would help fill in a blank in a memory otherwise clear-edged. As before, a sunset sky threw the Sasso into silhouette. The platform was crowded with troops moving off on some exercise. Their presence and a line of cattle trucks in a siding helped to carry me back vividly twenty years. I walked a little way beyond the platform along the track, visualizing the huddled shape beneath the sack and the protruding boots.

"More ghosts?" asked Matthew who had followed me. "You'd do much better to come and have that drink."

"A friend of mine was shot just over there. Why and how has always been a mystery. The Germans said he was trying to escape. There was a Court of Inquiry after the war. I didn't give evidence because I wasn't with him at the time but I looked at the War Office files some months ago. Several officers saw it happen and were definite that he was standing still—he may have drifted a few yards out of the queue. Perhaps they shot him deliberately—a warning to the rest of us. But I've always felt there was more to it. He'd been educated in England and had British nationality but his family, I believe, was half-German, half-Italian. When I last spoke to him he was worried what might happen if the Germans caught him. He'd joined a party of Yugoslavs, disguised in their uniform."

"Anyone I knew?"

"I don't think so. He was called Kempster."

"But—you can't mean Henry Kempster? I recruited him to the unit myself in Cairo." He was staring at me rather oddly.

"Oh, did you? I'd forgotten."

"I'd met his parents in Venice before the war. Their name was Von Kemperer, one of those cosmopolitan families, with relations all over Europe. The father was German but, when he died in the mid-thirties, his wife and daughter took Italian nationality—they lived between Venice and Florence mostly at that time. They were friends of my mother. She and Luke and I used to come to Italy a lot, as you know. When Henry asked to join Bomfrey's Boys in Cairo I tried to dissuade him. I knew it could be tricky if he was caught—for his family too. He was so keen that I gave in. After all, it was his own business and he was a useful man to have."

"Yes, he had plenty of guts. I owed him a lot, one way and another, but I was too young, or too English, to appreciate his problems. Actually he once gave me his sister's address in Florence. Of course I lost it. The name had something to do with a stomach, I remember. After the war I made a few inquiries, but not very hard, I'm afraid. Well, I've seen all I want to here. Now for that drink."

"I'm sure your Abruzzese have very beautiful characters," said Matthew, when we were sipping campari sodas beside the statue of long-nosed Ovid standing on a book. "But I can't say I think them much to look at. They're clumsily built and I haven't seen a single striking face, male or female. We might be in Belgium. Or for that matter Bolton."

A gay crowd milled down the main street past the little piazza, the same crowd that had barricaded the Prefect of L'Aquila in the Town Hall near us. Most appeared to be on their way to the fair in the Piazza Garibaldi, the sounds of which could be heard above the steady roar of motor scooters.

"I suppose not," I said. "I never really notice faces, only buildings. Look at the extraordinary *art-nouveau* front to that barber's shop," and I pointed to the word *Barbiere* supported by a languid motif of Walter Crane lilies. "How can it have got there? It must be the only thing of its kind in the whole Abruzzi. It's the sort of anomaly that Mark Duffy would appreciate."

"Meaning that it's wasted on me. I'm afraid it is. Wasn't Mark with you when you escaped?"

"Oh, yes. Mark was with us. Curious that the shop's open. Barbers usually close on Mondays in Italy. I suppose the *festa* . . ."

"Did he get through the lines with you?"

"No. He stayed in hiding till the Allies arrived the next summer. Then he fixed himself a marvelous job with Military Government—advising what works of art were to be salvaged and so forth. He had the time of his life, he told me afterwards."

A thin man, rather taller than the rest, had come out of the barber's shop and turned down the street towards the fair. The crowd blocked my view and I only caught a glimpse of him, but he wore some kind of uniform that might have been a *carabiniere*'s. His right

sleeve, I thought, was empty, pinned across the tunic. But perhaps
I'd imagined it.

"I ask," said Matthew, "because as it happens I was talking about
Mark the other day in Florence . . ."

"Oh yes?" I'd be able to overtake the man if I hurried and I
waved to the waiter for the bill. "Look," I said, "supposing you
spend an hour on the dodgems while I go and see my peasants?
There's bound to be a lot of reminiscing—awfully boring for you.
We'd meet back at the hotel for dinner."

As a rule Matthew hates being left alone for more than a minute.
He may travel in remote parts of the world, but always accompanied by a crowd of tribesmen, porters, or whatever and has probably
spent fewer hours over the last twenty years in total solitude than,
like most painters, I'm accustomed to spend in a week. However, he
said casually, "That would suit fine. I can put my call through. Let's
keep the dodgems till after dinner. Do you remember, at that lunch
party, rather a pretty woman sitting on my left?"

"Very well. She was much more than pretty and I wished she
was next to me instead of the gnädige Frau. She had what you call
a striking face . . ." I'd have to run now to catch the man before he
disappeared in the crowd on the Piazza Garibaldi.

"Did you think so?" Matthew sounded pleased. "I was talking
about Mark with her, actually. She had an affair with him at the end
of the war."

"Really? Would you mind settling the bill? If I wait for the waiter
I'll be here all night. See you at the hotel in about an hour."

As I left the table Matthew called out after me, "By the way, I
forgot to mention it, she's Henry Kempster's sister . . ."

"Counting motor-bikes as a half," said Amos, "I make it fifty-five
going north so far."

"Only seventeen going south," I said.

"They're on the run all right," said Mark.

It would have been about 10th October, at any rate two days
after our arrival at Gabriele's farm, and we were crouching in the
mouth of a cave on the hillside above. A carpet of lush fields separated us from the white streak of the Strada Nazionale that led south
from Sulmona to Castel di Sangro and Isernia. The road was the

Germans' central supply route to the Front and we hoped that a traffic census would give an indication of the battle's progress.

"Does it look good?" asked Dionino, Gabriele's nephew.

"Very good, Dionino," we said. "Let's have some of the bread and cheese you carried up. That looks even better."

The day before, Gabriele had held open court in the pigsty, presenting us, like all-too-reluctant debutantes, to a host of neighbors eager to meet the three *Inglesi*. "Your army will be here tomorrow!" they cried, one or two of them under the impression that we were its advance guard. Some brought gifts of food, others treasured garments of American manufacture, sent home in the past by luckier members of the family who had gone there and not been so foolish as to return. A young sailor, awaiting the Allied arrival in order to rejoin his family in Sicily, made the splendid gesture of pulling off his striped nautical shirt and handing it to Mark.

The sun shone, the general mood of optimistic gaiety exhilarated, and a little alarmed us. Two older visitors, Lorenzo the miller and one whom we knew simply as *il pastore*, shook their heads with a wiser caution. This premature rejoicing could be dangerous, they warned us. Gabriele was an irresponsible fellow whose good nature got the better of his judgment. There were no Germans in the immediate neighborhood but a *carabiniere* corporal slept in the next farm. They advised us to stay up on the mountain, at least in daylight. Accordingly we'd come up to the cave at dawn of the second day with Dionino as our guide. The proud owner of an American leather windbreaker, he was immensely friendly, like an overgrown retriever puppy, and he followed our conversation attentively, less from interest in the military situation than in order to improve his English against the happy time when he could migrate to the States.

At a much later period, when we tried to recall past incidents, we found that in retrospect whole weeks had blurred together, whereas certain isolated days remained vivid in every detail. This was one of those days, chiefly because of the oppressive boredom. For the first time we were faced with the necessity of spending a dozen hours on end with no distractions beyond those we could improvise. Counting German traffic was one distraction. When a small convoy passed heading north we cheered as loudly as we dared. When another passed the wrong way we groaned.

To while away the time Mark struggled to teach Dionino how to decline the verbs "to be" and "to have." "I suppose that to him I'm some sort of a god," he said. (We were all Thurber fans. It was perhaps our greatest bond.) In return Dionino promised to find us something to read. Anything, in any language, would do, we assured him. We craved for the printed page. He could not think of anyone locally who possessed a book but offered hope of a French Grammar that he believed his fiancée had pinched from school.

Personally I would have given a great deal for a pencil and paper. The sharp pattern of fields, each a different color and texture, the rows of poplars often set at an eccentric angle, the contrast between the cultivation and the bare face of Mt. Rotella opposite, all stirred impulses towards a kind of abstract painting that I had to wait many years to indulge.

The railway from Sulmona to the south ran through the cultivation on our side of the Strada Nazionale and parallel with it as far as the village of Pettorano at the head of the valley. From there it turned back, traversing the rocky face of Mt. Rotella on viaducts, and disappearing through a tunnel on its way south again past Campo di Giove (how did Jove come to have a field in the Abruzzi? We never learnt) to Roccaraso and Castel di Sangro. We played the same game with the trains as with the traffic. One passed in each direction about every couple of hours. There was little to be deduced from that. We wondered why the line, so visible and so vulnerable, had not been bombed by the R.A.F.

"I think you should consider trying to sabotage the viaducts," said Mark. "It's what Matthew Prendergast would do in your position."

"You might ask Gabriele to buy us thirty kilos of T.N.T.," I said, and the subject was not referred to again.

"A marvelous chap, Matthew," said Amos. "Not that I know him very well. We'd hardly met before the submarine depot ship in Algiers and I doubt if I ever would come to know him much better. The ruthless jaw and cold grey eyes rather unnerve me. But goodness, I admire his achievements. In war, so few people have the guts to carry out their own ideas, or have ideas worth carrying out. I suppose some day he'll be reckoned among the great guerrilla leaders."

Mark, in his high-pitched pedantic voice, said sharply, "No, no. That puts it altogether too high. A great guerrilla leader suggests a great contribution to a particular war, or a lone fight for a great cause. Matthew's been extremely daring and he and Oliver Bomfrey have shown considerable initiative. But one really can't pretend that Bomfrey's Boys have *contributed* anything out of the ordinary, except to give a lot of dashing young men a good excuse to escape soldiering."

"Well, that's not so little," said Amos. "And Bomfrey's Boys certainly livened things up in the desert at a time when G.H.Q. in Cairo was unimaginative and defeatist. They showed that the Germans could be *attacked*, even if we hadn't enough armor for a full-scale offensive. I agree that their *raison d'être* is less obvious now and that our operation in Sardinia was simply a waste of effort."

"Where do you imagine they are at present?" I said. "Some of them might turn up here, I suppose, if they haven't all gone to the Greek Islands. Matthew always went there on the slightest excuse."

"I wonder what he'll do after the war, if he survives."

"I doubt if he'll do anything much," said Mark. "He's the sort of person whom a war throws up—and then leaves high and dry."

"I think he'll travel," I said. "Before the war he once told me that that was his only real ambition. His mother was a friend of my mother's and I knew Matthew and his brother as boys. We rather hated one another then, but I became much fonder of Luke in Cairo. He was in Psychological Warfare and I spent the odd leave in his flat. He's a delightful donnish sort of person—something like you, Mark, but less prickly."

"Oh yes, I know Luke. We overlapped at Oxford. I'm not sure about the 'donnish.' He got a bad Second. In those days Matthew was just a rugger tough. He was engaged to my sister for a short time at the beginning of the war. She broke it off. I fancy he holds it against me. At least he scowled fiercely when he visited us in Athlit and found me there."

"I think you're imagining it," I said. "He wanted to marry my wife long before I did, but I'm sure he doesn't hold *that* against *me*. Rather the contrary. I doubt if he'll ever get married. Unless he finds someone as independent-minded as himself and they both go their separate ways most of the time."

"Perhaps in middle-age, when he's done what he wants to do," said Amos. "One gets sort of lonely. I may decide to marry again myself after the war. Incidentally, I thought Oliver Bomfrey wanted to marry your wife."

"Well, I don't know about *marriage*. But she had quite a few eligible suitors. None of her friends could ever understand why she settled on *me*."

"Oh, I can understand it. From what I've seen of her, she's an extremely capable girl with a highly developed maternal instinct. And frankly, before the war, you needed a nanny."

"Concentrate. You're not concentrating," said Mark. "Three more trucks passed going south, one north, and you were both too busy nattering to notice them. I have to do all the work."

"Concentrate? *Concentrare?*" asked Dionino.

"Good, Dionino. You're picking it up well. You'll be able to talk like anything to the Eighth Army when it arrives next week!"

That it would arrive we felt increasingly sure—our traffic census confirmed the optimism of Gabriele and his friends. But the valley was too risky, for them and for us. We'd decided to take the advice of Lorenzo the miller and *il pastore* and keep right out of the way. Dionino had told us that a British general was hiding in a cave three hours up the mountain. He and his uncle would take us to join the general next day with a supply of food for a week. His uncle was always glad of the excuse for a day's shooting.

"We don't want to stay up there longer than necessary," said Mark.

"Don't worry. We'll come and fetch you down instantly *quando arrivano gli Inglesi*. We'll have a *festa!*"

"By God we will," we said.

Towards evening the totals stood at a hundred and fifty-two German trucks passing north, only thirty-five passing south.

"It's an absolute rout," said Mark.

"What's that coming out of Sulmona now?" I said.

A long convoy had started to drive unconcernedly south along the Strada Nazionale. They were not even spaced out against air attack. After a hundred and fifty we gave up counting.

"Bugger!" said Amos.

CHAPTER XII

The higher up the mountain
the greener grows the grass . . .

according to a ribald ditty that Amos and I sang in our Yeomanry days. Certainly it was true of Genzana. On the lower reaches there was no grass at all and the tinder-dry scrub through which we climbed for the first hour offered scarcely enough grazing for a starved goat. It had been an exceptionally parched summer, Gabriele told us, and a disastrous harvest. He hoped the Allied army would bring plenty of food with it. Otherwise, when winter came . . . But he was a cheerful fellow by nature, free from the burden of creative pessimism, and he shrugged off these forebodings, evidently pleased to have a day away from the cares of the farm and, maybe, from the scoldings of his young wife.

To us she was bountiful as a goddess and had woken us in the pigsty with cups of hot sweetened sheep's milk, while her husband and Dionino loaded the donkey's wooden pack-saddle with such stores as they could spare us for the cave—a tattered blanket, an old Italian army cloak and water-bottle, a few apples and nuts, and a large flat loaf stuffed with peppers and gobbets of veal. As some sort of compensation we wrote out a testimonial, to be kept hidden till the Allies came. "To whom it may concern . . . This is to certify that Gabriele and his wife have sheltered and fed the three undersigned escaped British P.O.W.s . . ."

"I can but pray," said Amos, "that unlike most of my cheques this one won't bounce."

He and I were in a fever to get started, to reach the safety of the mountain. We had begun to feel trapped, to fear that every further minute in the valley tempted providence. But the preparations for departure dragged on. Mark began to grumble at the food supply. "What they've provided will only last three days at the most. We may be stuck up there for a week. I'm sure they'd give us more if we insisted. After all, we are paying for it, in a sense . . ."

Gabriele fetched a rusty single-barreled shotgun and a pock-etful of mildewed cartridges. "Is there much game up there?" we asked, doubtful that the weapon could do any damage if there was. He waved an arm grandiloquently. "Partridges, rabbits, hares . . . Always much to shoot on the mountain." His wife, cocking a skep-tical eye, bade him take an axe so that he could at least bring back some logs.

The sun was already too warm for comfort by the time we at last set off up the steep track, Dionino leading, Gabriele and the don-key in the rear. As climbs go it was not worth mentioning but we made heavy weather of it. Amos's and Mark's sandshoes gave little protection against the sharp stones and thorns, the soles of my boots were full of holes and coming unstitched. Gradually the grey tow-ers of Sulmona fell away behind the mountain's flank, the white rib-bon of the Strada Nazionale turned to a thread of cotton, and the cultivation below on our left assumed ever more and more abstract patterns.

"How much farther is the cave?" panted Mark after an hour and a half, when we stopped for a rest near the upper edge of the scrub.

"Not far, not far. Another half-hour," said Dionino, still full of breath.

Gabriele, with the incurable optimism of the true sportsman, slipped a cartridge into his gun. We made so much noise that any game must have fled our approach and in fact we saw nothing more than a goldfinch which he fired at and missed. An hour later we were well out of the scrub and on to a smooth shoulder where a breeze freshened us. The mountain appeared to end a few hundred feet higher, against a blazing sky. We sat a while among the stunted stems of wild lavender, looking down a long way now on to the railway viaducts of Mt. Rotella, though its peak was still far above us. Beyond it the Maiella spread out in its full immensity.

"Many *Inglesi* hiding there," laughed Gabriele. "Many, many."

"What about this general at our cave? Did you see him?"

"Not myself, but I heard he was there last week. The cave is safe. Only shepherds know of it and they are still right up on Genzana, at the three *fontane*."

"How much farther to the cave?" asked Mark.

"Not far, not far," said Dionino. "Another half-hour."

The earth round us had been cultivated in the past, the ridge and furrow still showed through the dried grass. Gabriele remembered his father ploughing it, in the days when more peasants lived in the valley and more land had been needed. "Now all leave who can." He sighed. "In those days there were many more partridges and hares up here, but they have left also."

To cheer him, we threw stones in the air for him to shoot at. "Won't your wife ask what's happened to all the cartridges?"

"I shall take her plenty of logs instead."

A single fig tree, a relic of the earlier cultivation, still survived. We found a dozen black figs on it, small and sweet, which we gratefully ate before continuing. As always, the summit turned out to be merely a crest, but from it we could see the true peak, still about three miles away and at least two thousand feet higher. Mark groaned. "Oh, God, don't say the cave is up there!"

"No, no, it is in a little valley on this side, among the trees. You can just see their tops."

"About half an hour more?"

"Yes, about half an hour."

We all laughed. The air was fresher, we had got our second wind and were enjoying the climb, imagining ourselves real mountaineers. A deep gorge appeared on our left, leading back towards the Gizio Valley, to Pettorano itself. "That's a better way up," they explained. "An easier zigzag. But more dangerous. People would see you—and know you were here."

We converged on the top of the gorge, where it widened into a grassier upper valley with beeches, and to reach it traversed a long shaly slope. Our feet slipped continually and we slithered across, steadying ourselves on bushes of beech scrub. The trees grew larger, not large by English parkland standards but some of them thirty feet tall, their roots giving a better foothold on the shale. A last hundred yards of scrambling and we were at a small outcrop of limestone, beneath which lay a cave so tiny that we might have passed within ten yards without noticing it. We had been climbing for four hours.

"By God," said Mark, flopping on to the edge of turf at the cave mouth. "I wouldn't do that climb again if you gave me a thousand pounds!"

But he did.

Mark christened it *Little Ease*, after the dungeon in the Tower. Really it was no more than a scallop-shaped cavity under the rock, perhaps four feet at its highest point, five feet in depth, and wide enough for the three of us to lie down with a foot to spare on either side. Gabriele apologized for the absence of any general, but there were traces of recent occupation. Among the leaves on the stony floor we found two potatoes and five walnuts for which we were soon to be thankful.

As a hide-up it was almost ideal, tucked among the beeches on the near-precipitous hillside and about a hundred feet above the valley's grassy bed. We could see as far as the mouth of the gorge in one direction, in the other to the valley's upper end, where it debouched on to the ridge of Genzana. Anyone coming up from Pettorano or down from the high sheep pastures would be visible for half a mile before he reached us. And although someone might approach the cave unseen through the trees, we should at least hear his footsteps on the shale some distance off. All we needed was water. Dionino offered to lead me up to the nearest *fontana* while Mark and Amos built a fire at the cave mouth and Gabriele chopped logs to take home.

The beech forest extended round three sides of Genzana's bald crown like a tonsure. Dionino and I climbed through it, following the slope of the valley and meeting no one, though we passed a disused sheep-pen made from rope-netting and a deserted charcoal-burner's hut. After an hour, we emerged on to the crown itself at the *fontana*, the spring water carefully piped into a trough. There were few tracks on the turf round it. The flocks, Dionino thought, must be beyond, at the second or third *fontana*. The shepherds were keeping out of the Germans' way as long as possible.

We admired a view of mountains in all directions. Our own range extended past the peak of Genzana out of sight to the south. Mark's map, which I'd brought with me, was too small in scale to give more than a rough idea of distances, but it mentioned the villages of Alfedena and Villetta Barrea on the River Sangro which, I calculated, must be about twenty miles away in a straight line. But mileage on a map means nothing in mountains. How long would it take to walk to the villages? I asked Dionino. He made a face. He had never been to them, had never, indeed, been farther from home than this *fontana*. It would take—oh, days and days. Three, at any rate, he supposed, if you were so mad as to attempt it and if you had food and tough boots and knew the route. There was a valley to be crossed he believed—somewhere above the Plain of Cinquemiglia. He begged me not even to think of such a course. We would be safe in the cave. He and his uncle would carry up more food, if the Allied army still hadn't come in four or five days. It was expected to reach the Sangro at any moment—one of his friends had heard it announced on the wireless the night before. As if confirming the rumor a distant rumble echoed across the mountains. Guns, said Dionino. Or thunder? No, no, definitely guns!

The map marked Scanno and its lake below us to the west somewhere. We could see the mountains on the far side of the valley of the Sagittario, that flowed from the lake round the north of Genzana, to join the Gizio near Sulmona. *Il professore* had mentioned the Sagittario Gorge, one of the great sights of the Abruzzi (or of anywhere— Lear, no mean judge, who rode up it on horseback, described it as the wildest freak of nature he had ever seen). I longed to walk a few hundred yards nearer and peep over, but the sky had suddenly misted. The *fontana* stood at 5500 feet, a thousand feet higher than *Little Ease*, we were threatened suddenly with dense cloud and hastened back. We found Amos and Mark crouched over a fire. Gabriele, his donkey half-buried under logs, waited impatiently to be off. "We will return in four days without fail," he promised.

"Or sooner, if the Allies come before!" cried Dionino gaily.

They took the easier route down by Pettorano and as we watched them disappear Amos said, "I've just realized we have no matches. We'll have to be bloody careful to keep this fire going."

The cloud thickened in our little valley, a damp white fog that dripped off the beeches and cut visibility to a yard or two. We began to learn how unprepared we were for existence at this height and in what was virtually the open. We had no chopper, not even a knife. Such loose wood as we could find was sodden and burnt badly. We dared not venture far in search of better for fear of missing the way back. We took it in turns to keep the fire going through the night, not that we slept much. The cave floor did not permit of scooping a hollow for the hip bone. The blanket, cloak, and greatcoat were utterly inadequate against the cold that crept round every inch of our bodies, and set our teeth chattering for hours on end. For once Mark's flow of conversation dried up completely. He complained, merely, that we should have remained below in the valley at all costs.

During the second night he let the fire go out. We'd finished the loaf and peppers by then, also our water. On the third morning the cloud lifted for an hour or two and, to make amends, he volunteered to refill the bottle at the *fontana*. When he'd left, Amos said, "I hate to run anyone down behind his back but your friend Mark is the most impossibly selfish bastard I've ever met. Otherwise he's a nice enough chap."

When he returned, we found he had managed to lose the bottle's cork and half the water had spilled. We drank what remained. The gobbets of veal had gone bad, but we smashed the Canadian tin of meat open on a rock. In the afternoon the cloud lifted again and Amos went up to the *fontana*. "Your friend is a nice enough chap," said Mark. "Otherwise he strikes me as the most impossibly selfish bastard I've ever met."

Doubtless they said exactly the same about me when I refilled the bottle on the fourth day.

There was no sign of Gabriele and Dionino. We shared the walnuts and raw potatoes meticulously. "If we'd had the sense to bring a billycan," said Amos, "we could have boiled the potatoes. If we'd had a fire."

The cloud settled thicker than ever. On the fifth day also. There was nothing left to eat and we were too weak to climb to the *fontana*. We were too weak to descend again to Gabriele's farm, either, but we agreed to make the attempt the following day whatever happened. It was the only thing we did agree on. We were past speaking.

None of us were the sort of men who in normal circumstances came to blows, but now such painful measures were the matter of ever recurring speculation as we lay huddled together in a perpetual white night, silently hating one another. We were thus huddled when, about ten o'clock on the sixth day, voices sounded close by and there, peering in at us through the mist, was Dionino with an older man and two girls.

"Sorry we couldn't get here sooner," said Dionino, or to that effect. "The Germans raided my uncle's farm—we believe the *carabiniere* corporal tipped them off. They nearly shot Gabriele but when they could find no trace of you they only took his pigs."

"What's the news of the Allied army?"

"It will be here definitely in a week. Last night the radio said it had reached Isernia."

"Isernia! But it got there a fortnight ago."

Dionino introduced the stranger, a powerfully-built peasant of fifty called Antonio, his face grizzled and impassive. He had fought against the Germans in the first war, and been to America for a short time afterwards. He spoke no English, indeed was a man of few words of any sort but with, obviously, a kind heart—how kind, we came to know well enough. Hearing of us from Dionino, who was engaged to one of his daughters, Antonio had decided to take us over. It was too difficult, Dionino explained on his behalf, to go on bringing food up to the cave. A safe place had been found in the valley, we would go down there at dusk.

Antonio's two fine daughters, built on a heroic, indeed somewhat bovine, model, had carried up a large earthenware dish of macaroni, covered with a cloth and still fairly hot. They sat shivering in the cave mouth while we devoured it. They wore nothing much more against the weather than a shift, but evidently were used to it. We tried to be polite to them, to express a fraction of the gratitude we felt, but they were girls of even fewer words than their father, and (now and in the future) appeared not to hear what we were saying and not to care. Antonio himself was always embarrassed by our thanks. In reply he would wave a hand at whatever dish he had provided and say gruffly, "*Non importa ringraziare, mangiare*," or something of the kind, which in any case meant "Get on and eat it while it's hot."

The meal finished, the fire re-lit, Dionino told us he had been leading a life of hairbreadth escapes from the Germans, and from the unknown fate which befell any *giovanotto* whom they caught. "*Sempre scappare...*" He had been continually "scapparying" by the skin of his teeth, but such was his devotion to ourselves and to the Allies that he held his personal safety of no account. All he wanted was to help us. We had other friends as well, he said, pulling out a letter from the pocket of his leather windbreaker and handing it over.

It read as follows:

Dear Sirs,

I am a British subject in hiding from the Germans. It is both my duty and my desire to render you assistance. I am in touch with two British generals, living in the valley, who are anxious to have your names. I hope this tin of meat and this dagger will be useful to you. You can use the dagger for opening the tin.

God save the King! Rule, Britannia!

Your humble servant,
Frank Del Signore

p.s.—The glorious Eighth Army has definitely taken Campobasso, is advancing rapidly on Isernia and should be in Sulmona shortly.

Dionino had forgotten to bring the tin of meat and the dagger, but told us we should meet the flamboyant-sounding Frank that evening. He had little else to say about this intriguing new friend of whom, clearly, he was in awe.

At evening we set off by the route we had come, fervently hoping that we would not have to make the ascent ever again. The clouds had lifted, the night was dark but starlit, and we reached the Gizio Valley in three hours. Antonio's house stood in open fields on a track near the railway line, half a mile farther from Sulmona than Gabriele's farm. He and his daughters went in first to be sure that all was well, while we and Dionino lurked behind a haystack. A daughter came out again and conducted us up a wide stone staircase into an attic, its windows heavily shuttered, and bare of furniture save for a small table and half a dozen chairs. Maize cobs lay heaped in one corner, sacks of grain in another, bacon flitches and strings of onions hung from a beam. The attic smelt pleasantly of flour. To heighten the conspiratorial atmosphere there was no light except a candle on the table, its flame casting strange shadows on the white-washed stone walls. Waiting for us in the loft, besides Antonio, we found a debonair Bertie Wooster-ish young man of perhaps thirty, smartly dressed in a plus-four suit of dark brown tweed and wearing a trilby hat of palest fawn. He introduced himself in fluent English, and with an early-Victorian style of politeness, as Frank Del Signore, our humble servant.

"What a pleasure to meet someone civilized again, at last," said Mark.

Antonio's wife, a superb gipsified Dorelia by Augustus John, and as taciturn as her husband, brought in a wine bottle and glasses and a platter with steaming lumps of pork fat. While we ate and drank, Frank quickly gave us his story. His grandfather had been an Abruzzese sculptor who went to live in England towards the end of the last century; some sort of relation, he said, of Dante Gabriel Rossetti, whose own father, Gabriele, had migrated there as a political refugee fifty years before that. Frank himself was brought up partly in England and owned a British passport, but for reasons that never became clear he returned to Italy in the thirties, to work in films. On the outbreak of war he was interned, and pressed to renounce his British nationality and join the Italian army. He showed us a scar on his calf where an Italian sergeant, as part of the pressure, had prodded him with a bayonet. But Frank resisted all such persuasions and remained loyal to the British Crown. He was released because of his poor health and after various wanderings had come to live quietly with his sister on a farm nearby, waiting for the Allies. "My body is fragile, my spirit indomitable," he said, striking his chest and coughing. He was helping any escaped P.O.W. he could contact, among them the two generals he had mentioned in his letter who were on another farm not far away and whom we agreed to meet as soon as possible.

Frank boasted rather naïvely of his efforts to stir up local resistance to the Germans. But—and he shrugged his shoulders—he was ashamed to say that he could do nothing with such people.

They were all stupid and cowardly. Otherwise, he inferred, there might have been continual attacks on the Strada Nazionale and the railway line, even a wholesale massacre of the German detachments billeted in the countryside . . .

Antonio and Dionino listened with evident envy to this high-speed and unintelligible display of English, and with, we could see, some misgivings about Frank himself. We understood their doubts better when we learnt that Frank's sister was married to the same *carabiniere* corporal whom they suspected of having betrayed Gabriele to the Germans. Frank made no secret of his feelings about his brother-in law. "A great big Fascist *brute*," he said. "A bully. I never could understand what my sister saw in him. A *low* sort of person. I find him most—most *uncongenial* to me!"

We were delighted with Frank. Delicate in health and still suffering from his ill-treatment by the Fascists, he was something of a *mythomane* whose exaggerations need not be believed but who, we rightly guessed, was entirely to be trusted. "We English must stick together," he said many times.

"Surely you are running a great risk as an Englishman dressed as an Italian and doing what you are?" we said, trying not to smile. "Please be extremely careful."

Frank dismissed the danger with a reckless laugh. "I can take care of myself." He revealed the pistol that he always carried in a pocket of the plus-fours and with which, if it came to the worst, he hoped to account for a few Germans before going under. It was all part of an act, which became familiar enough. We made affectionate fun of him. But he ran appalling risks, real or imaginary, on our account and besides much else we had to thank him for a reasonably accurate supply of B.B.C. news. Looking back, I can't imagine why he, or anyone else, bothered with us for a moment. There was nothing at all to be gained by doing so, everything to lose. In Frank's case Patriotism was enough. "God save the King!" he said, and slipped away into the night whistling "The British Grenadiers."

By then we were pleasantly drunk, and even more happily optimistic about our future. Contact with British generals, regular B.B.C. news from Frank, the inspiring friendliness of Antonio . . . Our circumstances had indeed taken an unexpected turn for the better. Dionino explained that Antonio's house was too exposed for us to stay in. He and his future father-in-law led us by a track a short distance to the back of a farmhouse built right against the mountain. A small figure emerged from the shadows to take us over.

Owing to the slope, the farm's top story could be entered from ground level. Our new host opened a hatch under the eaves and ushered us into a loft. We collapsed on to sweet-smelling hay, softer and warmer than any bed we had dreamt of.

"I believe we're dead and have gone to Heaven," said Amos.

Before the hatch closed the voice of an Archangel, or maybe of God himself, spoke from the outer darkness, a cheerful staccato kind of voice, but of great gentleness and burred with a slight American accent.

"Them Germany bastards not come here. You fellers sleep O.K. I guess. Well, I leave you now. G'night."

CHAPTER XIII

HIS FULL NAME was Sinibaldo Amatangelo. In the district of Pettorano sul Gizio, where his family had lived for as many generations as he could be bothered to count back, he was known affectionately as Baldo. We called him Sam, the name he had used in the States where he migrated as a laborer for a while in the twenties. He was Antonio's best friend, eight years or so younger, and a good deal poorer.

It was hard to see how he would ever become any richer. He was a skilled and thrifty farmer, he squeezed all that could be squeezed from the half-dozen acres of stony soil and their sprinkling of vines, olives, and fruit trees. The land, like the house, belonged to him, freehold, but it lay scattered in separate strips for a mile across the foot of the mountain. The farmyard had a small well but the nearest irrigation channel ran several hundred yards lower down, past Antonio's house, and Sam had to water his crops laboriously by hand. He grew wheat for his bread, barley for his livestock—a cow, a pig, some chickens, and a donkey—and maize for them all. In a good year he, his wife, and three teenage sons fed well, and were able to store something against a bad year. He kept his own seed for sowing and paid for certain other essentials by barter—the grinding of his corn or taking his cow to the bull. But, like most of their neighbors, he and his family were never far from starvation and there was devilish little surplus that could be sold, to buy tools, or fresh stock, or clothes.

He only possessed the one old pair of grey worsted knee-breeches, hitched up by a strong leather belt on which he carried a knife and billhook, and the one tweed coat, much patched. He did his own darning, as he mended his only pair of boots. For he liked to do things for himself, and do them *well*. The sort of man—it might serve as the definition of an artist—who hated the slipshod and couldn't bear not to finish whatever job he undertook. He could turn his hand to everything, to killing and curing a pig, to fashioning a wooden plough, to making salami. In appearance he was ordinary enough, a small wiry nimble man, his face not at all what Matthew would call striking, but round and rubbery and slightly comical, rather child-like in its innocence and with the kindest and most patently *honest* pair of blue eyes I've ever seen. When this book is filmed, I do so hope his part won't be played by Gregory Peck.

Antonio we liked and admired. Heaven knows we owed him more than could ever be repaid. But he was a difficult man to understand, deeply reserved, and shut off further from us by a peasant cunning that often seemed at variance with his palpable generosity. Sam we *loved*.

We loved him from the start, from the moment we saw him in daylight on the first morning. The house was three-storied, each floor having an entrance at ground-level. Inside, a ladder led down from the hay-loft, through the kitchen and bedroom on the first floor, to the stable below. He had climbed the ladder and his head, in the greasy old cap he habitually wore, bobbed up unexpectedly in the hay at our feet. "You fellers sleep O.K.? I bring you some milk. Freshen you up, I guess!"

He'd learnt about twenty words of English in the States, but he managed to say more with them than most of us do with a vocabulary a hundred times greater. Now, when we had exchanged greetings, he blazed with indignation at the Germans for stealing Gabriele's pigs. "That's not right, them Germany sons of bitches take them feller's pigs. Not *right*. Them feller has to live, same as everyone. Without his pigs, them feller starve this winter."

"It was all because of us, too," we said. "We'll see that he is repaid—when our Army comes. We can promise that much, at least."

Sam's anger could be withering but it never lasted. He was essentially a happy man, bubbling with fun and with a keen, but tolerant, eye for his neighbors' follies. Suddenly he laughed, enjoying a side to the situation that we could hardly appreciate. In his chirpy singsong idiom, he added, "You fellers not to blame that Gabriele talk. Him tell peoples that him look after three Englishmen. Him tell everyone. Now him sad. His wife very angry—aye, aye. Very angry with *him*! But I bring her some of my pig. Now she not so angry. And him lucky them Germany peoples not shoot him. That feller not talk so much again."

"I'm afraid he won't, poor devil," said Amos. "Does he know that we're here?"

Sam shook his head and became serious. "*Nobody* must know that. It's lucky, that Antonio and I find you. Other peoples round here different. Some tell, maybe. But we feed you fellers. You stay here safely till your peoples come."

"Sam, we'll do whatever you say. We don't know how to thank you . . ."

"Ah, that's nothing." He waved a hand to forestall compliments. "You're welcome. I like to help you fellers. My wife making a min-estra for you now. Like this—I tell her how." He gestured expres-sively to explain the way it should be done. "Chop up them peppers first, see? Small—my finger. Fry them in a little pork fat. One min-ute, perhaps two . . ." He was a wonderful cook and often talked lyrically of the proper herbs to mix with sausage meat, of the right way to roll and cut up *pasta*, of his method of preserving cherries or peaches in brandy . . . He described many basic recipes which, for a while after the war, I used to badger my wife to copy—till she got fed up. I fancy that Sam's wife got fed up too at times, for, if he had a fault, it was to try to do too much. She was a quiet, sensitive woman who suffered badly from asthma and was shy of strangers, so that we saw little of her or of the sons whom, for her sake, he kept out of the danger as far as possible. "I am a little worried for them, not for myself," Sam once admitted. Otherwise he showed only an embarrassing concern for *us*, and *our* comfort, cluck-clucking like a doting nanny over the mess we'd got ourselves into. "That's not right, you fellers living this way"—but that was at a much later period.

For the first couple of days we stayed happily in the loft. Antonio visited us, bringing, as well as food, another old army cloak, a ruck-sack, and a scribbled message from Frank Del Signore. "Regret can't see you in person. My brother-in-law being *very* difficult. I think he suspects. The glorious Eighth Army has definitely taken Isernia. God save the King."

Dionino also scrambled up the ladder, beaming with the excitement of his adventures, "*Sempre scapare...*" He produced Frank's dagger and tin of meat, also the promised French Grammar, a pitifully tattered volume containing mostly lists of verbs and pronouns and such like. However it did include, as translation exercises, short fables of a moral nature that we read aloud. One concerned an officious bluebottle that buzzed round the head of a carthorse pulling a heavy load uphill, saying, "Gracious, what hard work this is!" When the carthorse reached the top, the bluebottle exclaimed, "We managed that rather well, I thought!" Mark couldn't understand why Amos and I burst out laughing.

Early on the third morning Sam appeared suddenly in a state of barely controlled panic. The Germans were searching the farms for *giovanotti*, livestock, English prisoners, no one could be sure what. All the men in the valley were escaping up the mountain. He hurried us out of the hatch, showed us the track, and bade us stop up there out of sight till dusk. He said he intended to hide his cow and pig in a cave in the fields nearby and would follow later if he could. It was characteristic of him that, even in such circumstances, he had troubled to stuff a loaf with peppers which he put into our rucksack, as well as a bottle of wine.

The German troops at this time were mostly concentrated in Sulmona and a few neighboring villages like Intradacqua. They had not yet begun to occupy farms as a precaution against air attack. The sight of a soldier on a motor-bike, driving along one of the country lanes, was liable to be interpreted as a round-up and start a general rush for the mountain. We found ourselves among a host of *giovanotti* and older peasants, calling cheerfully to one another as they toiled up the track. The night before Sam had insisted on shaving off our beards, fearing that they made us too conspicuous, though we had rather fancied impressing the Eighth Army with them. Now we were thankful that he had, hoping to escape notice among the rest as we squatted among them in the scrub where they sat all day, chattering like starlings. However, Lorenzo the miller and *il pastore* both strolled across to our bush at one point, the former to give us some apples, the latter with a pocket-knife—a kindly

gesture that had repercussions. And when Antonio came in search
of us at midday, he was quickly directed to the three *Inglesi*. He was
accompanied by his little son, Manfredo, a sturdy handsome boy of
eight—and as silent as himself.

Antonio never saw us without giving us a present. Now he had
brought a pot of his own delicious honey and thrust it gruffly at us
with a simple and moving gesture, something like that of a man
offering his hand to another man after a quarrel. The gesture represented more than just a generous impulse and seemed to echo
a remote period, far older even than the Abruzzi, when Man first
struggled to emerge from savagery by clinging to a rigid code of hospitality. With Manfredo crouching at his feet, an archetypal Father
and Son, Antonio stayed silently with us on the hillside all afternoon, watching to see that we enjoyed the honey—which indeed we
did. He pressed us to drink occasionally from his flask of wine, slyly
asking if we didn't find it better than Sam's. The two friends were
devoted but also, we soon realized, a little jealous. They were utterly
contrasted characters. Sam, with all his poverty, was essentially no
different from ourselves, a modern man—bustling and matter of
fact, someone who believed that all obstacles could be overcome by
hard work and intelligence. Antonio was primeval.

The danger, if there had been any, receded. Towards evening the
mountainside emptied into the valley, and Sam himself arrived, to
lead us discreetly back to the farm.

His wife had prepared a meal for us which we ate in the kitchen
behind closed shutters, by candle light. That our presence was placing a strain on the household we knew, but preferred to ignore. Now
the evidence of the strain stared us in the face and put us to shame.
Sam's wife could not hide her anxiety and sobbed throughout the
meal; he himself looked exhausted with worry—though he pressed
second helpings on us with his usual solicitude; and we were on edge
that we could be seen by anyone peeping through the cracked shutters. Outside intermittent firing went on in the valley round us and,
although its cause was probably no more sinister than *giovanotti*
having their fun, the shots increased the tension. We were thankful
to withdraw to the darkness and security of the loft.

As we lay awake discussing the day's excitements, Amos said,
"You must do what you like but I can't stop here sponging off these

marvelous people any further. I intend to start walking tomorrow." The usual argument developed. I, too, longed to be off; Mark wanted to stay. But after a little he agreed that if the Allies were still only at Isernia they could not be expected to arrive for weeks.

"I can't let you two half-wits wander off on your own," he said. "If you absolutely insist on going, then I'll come."

"Thank God you're civilized enough to give way once in your life," said Amos. We were growing quite attached to Mark.

In the morning we'd ask Sam to spare us what he could. With the rucksack and extra cloak and *il pastore*'s knife we were now better equipped for the mountains and at least we knew the route as far as the first *fontana*. There was a great sense of relief in having reached a decision. "We'll set off as soon after dawn as we can," we said.

Mark and I were woken sooner than that by a convulsive shuddering in the hay between us, by a gasping moaning sound coming from Amos. His teeth chattered, he was dripping with sweat and his forehead was almost too hot to touch. He was in the throes of a high malarial fever.

The fever lasted three days. Amos lay in the loft, covered with the blanket, cloaks, and greatcoat and nursed by Sam. There were continual scares, but no Germans came closer than Gabriele's farm. To appease Mrs. Sam's very reasonable fears, Mark and I crept out of the hatch at dawn and stayed on the hillside till nightfall which by now was about 5 P.M. At Sam's request we tried to avoid all contact with anyone but, if met and questioned, said we were passing through the district on our way south and knew no one locally. It was the least we could do.

At night Sam locked the hatch as a further precaution. If we needed to relieve ourselves, we climbed down the ladder to the stables. One evening I was squatting there in the dark between the cow and the donkey when, from outside the closed doors, I heard someone softly whistling "The British Grenadiers." Frank was up in the loft when I got back. Having heard about Amos's malaria through Dionino, he had brought a bottle of quinine pills stolen from his brother-in-law. "I expect he will beat my sister when he finds they're missing," he said. "But if you marry a Fascist brute what else can you expect?"

Apart from that, he had come in order to conduct one of us to the two generals. As I'd been to Intradacqua, Mark claimed his turn. Sam, with misgivings, opened the hatch and Frank led the way. "You need have no fear," he said to Mark, drawing the pistol from the pocket of his plus-fours. "I shall walk a few paces in front."

There had been, we later learnt, a special prison for generals in Sulmona where about ten, some rather famous from the Desert campaigns, were confined with their batmen in a villa. After the Armistice one or two walked for it, the rest split up among peasant families. Mark, when Frank returned him safely around 10 P.M., gave us an amusing description of these two, whom I may as well call by his nickname, Marshall and Snelgrove. They and their batmen, all dressed as peasants, were sharing in the family life, and he had watched them kissing the babies good night. The house stood in a village where everyone was related and with a well-organized system of warning. If Germans approached, all the men took to the fields with the cattle. Marshall and Snelgrove confirmed that the Allies had just reached Isernia and thought we would be liberated in a fortnight at most. They kindly suggested to Mark that we join them in the village, where they knew of another family who would look after us.

It was a tempting offer. Although the village lay in the valley near Sulmona, without our line of retreat up the mountain, to go there would free Sam of the burden of us and we would be nearer a doctor if Amos's condition grew worse. But Sam, when we put it to him late that night, was so hurt and indignant that we regretted having even thought of it. And the next afternoon Frank, considerably shaken, slipped up to see us with the news that the Germans had just raided the village and seized most of the *giovanotti* and cattle, though Marshall and Snelgrove and their batmen had managed to escape. A bigger scare than ever started.

While Sam was quickly hiding his cow and pig in the same nearby cave, his wife came to the loft and begged us to go *away*. Poor dear, we knew she was right. But go where? To walk far with Amos was out of the question. The fever was down but he could hardly stand. Sam at first refused to let us leave but at length, seeing we were adamant, suggested another cave a mile up the mountain track, where he could still reach us and where we would be safe enough. With him as guide, we set off at first light. Amos rode the donkey, his legs trailing the ground. "It's like the good old days in the Barsetshire Yeomanry," he said.

"Adullam . . . Well, I *should* know, but just off-hand . . ."

"Something to do with the Arabian Nights?" suggested Amos.

"Adullam and the Forty Thieves . . ." Mark chuckled at our ignorance. "God, you are the most amazing advertisement for your old school. Your parents spent a fortune on your education but what did you both *learn*?"

"Quite a lot," I said. "Not least, how to forget inessentials."

"We learnt," said Amos, "what your school, in spite of its motto, never does seem able to teach anyone—that manners makyth man. Anyway, come off it. What *was* the Cave of Adullam?"

"'And every one that was in distress, and every one that was in debt, and every one that was discontented, gathered unto him . . .' At least that's roughly how it goes, but you see how applicable it is, especially the 'in debt.' David. Think of *David*. Now there really *was* a guerrilla leader, one of the great mythical figures of military history. Of course Adullam was far larger than this—a sort of fortress. At that stage of his life he was simply a brigand chief, combining Matthew's daring and Oliver's guile—and the hell of a lot besides. To put it another way you could call him Marco Sciarra and Torquato Tasso rolled into one and multiplied by ten. Consider his achievement. He raised a band of four hundred toughs. The Philistines, as you will doubtless recall . . ."

"Your point is taken," said Amos. "Spare us the lecture. The intellectual stimulus will only bring on my malaria again . . ."

The lower reaches of Genzana were riddled with caves. We got to know a dozen, of which Adullam was the largest and most romantic, in shape an apsidal dome fifteen feet high at its mouth, with a smooth floor of rock and a slightly raised platform at the back where we slept. There were even three convenient hollows on the platform for our hipbones. We took refuge there about 20th October. It lay in a dell on the steepest part of the hill, well screened by trees which did not prevent a view of the Strada Nazionale several hundred feet below and of the railway line on Mt. Rotella opposite. Thanks to the quinine pills, Amos began to regain strength, but the stone bed was bitterly cold and he was liable to break into violent shivering fits. When that happened Mark and I had literally to heap ourselves on top of him to restore warmth.

But life in Adullam was not uncomfortable, if dull. By day we had a companion in the form of a large black snake that sunned its beautiful gleaming body on a rock by the cave mouth for hours on end, rustling away like lightning into the scrub when the sun went in or if we disturbed it. Once Antonio, visiting us in day-time, saw it. He picked up a stone to throw, then put the stone down and sat silently regarding the snake for a minute. "Many snakes in the Abruzzi," he said. "Not dangerous." It was about the longest speech he'd ever made.

At night we built a small fire, keeping it hidden by means of a Heath Robinson arrangement of blankets suspended from the roof. I amused myself doing a charcoal caricature of ourselves, with our matted hair and beards, on the cave wall; also an anatomically freakish nude on another part of the surface that suggested the *motif.* For the rest we took a census of the traffic—with the same inconclusive results; set ourselves general knowledge tests; made plans for the ideal life after the war; or just talked.

Goodness, how we talked.

We talked of politics and religion, of State versus private education, of the case for nationalizing coal and the railways, of the Abdication, of mnemonics, of *Lady Chatterley's Lover*, of Oscar Wilde, of phlebotomy. We talked of our parents, our school days, our love affairs and youthful scrapes. Amos talked of his three marriages, and his only child, a daughter who had died soon after birth. I talked of my one marriage, and of the son I had not seen. We talked, on one occasion, of the importance of emotion in the creative process.

"I'm not sure that art has much to do with strong feelings," said Mark. "Black and white by themselves can't make a picture. The subtlety (as Delacroix said) is in the amount of grey. The same with literature. The strongest feelings can't be expressed in words—just in grunts and groans and shrieks. Literature is really about indecision, hesitation, doubt. 'To be or not to be' and all that. You see, all art is a fake. It's a *pretense* at strong emotions. Like the theater. In fact the art lies in the pretense. A photograph of an actual bleeding crucified Christ wouldn't be art. An actual raving Othello wouldn't be art. He *pretends* to rave. The words he uses are not the sort of words anyone in that condition would possibly use."

"So you mean real life hasn't anything to do with art?" I asked, a trifle mystified.

"Not with the arts. The only literature of real life is History. Look. If you're kicked on the shins you say 'Ow.' If you see a woman you madly want to sleep with you say 'Wow!' But if you're not sure how much you are hurt, or whether the woman has a husband who may be jealous, you write a book."

"*Are* there husbands these days who kick up a fuss?" said Amos, half asleep. "*I* never have."

"I wouldn't know," said Mark. "Personally I prefer boys. Better ask John. He's the happily married man."

"Well, I was once. But it seems a long time . . ."

Sam and Antonio took it in turns to visit us every day with food and water. They were cheerful but obviously living in hourly dread of being raided by the Germans. Sam kept his cow and pig permanently in the cave near his farm. Antonio's house was more vulnerable. He shrugged his shoulders. "If they come, they come." His deep-sunk eyes were expressionless but I couldn't help thinking that, if I was a German, I'd rather not find myself alone with Antonio in a dark corner.

They did come; or rather one soldier came. And Antonio was out—bringing a hot meal to *us*. He'd left all his money with his wife in a wallet. She stuffed the wallet in her dress where the marauding soldier spotted it—and took it. It contained about £50 worth of *lire*—his life's savings, we believed, though Sam, who told us the story next day, not without a certain grim amusement in his blue eyes, assured us that old Antonio had some more hidden elsewhere.

We were, simply, appalled. If Antonio had not been away bringing us food the whole thing would not have happened. He reported the theft to the German H.Q. in Sulmona but of course the soldier was never identified or the wallet found. To try to make the disaster seem a little less, we wrote out another "cheque," promising that the sum, like so much else, would be repaid *quando arrivano gli Inglesi*. But neither the loss, nor the promise, appeared to alter Antonio's feelings towards ourselves by one fraction of a degree. He brought us another hot meal the following evening as usual. *"Non importa ringraziare, mangiare!"*

"I can but pray," said Amos, "that Sam and Antonio secretly regard us as a sound financial investment. Otherwise what they're doing is inhuman."

It was to become far far more inhuman yet.

Our presence in the cave was not so secret as we supposed. Lorenzo the miller called in one day with a present of apples and nuts. "That's not much," Sam said indignantly when we told him. "Them feller rich. He should bring something hot for you." Lorenzo's wife, he added, was notoriously mean.

But most of his neighbors fell short of Sam's exacting standards. Gabriele was a generous enough fellow but a chatterbox who let his wife bully him. *Il pastore*, he said, was another who could have afforded to do more than give us a knife—which, moreover, he apparently now wanted *back*! Sam chuckled. "I say to him, 'If you not want them fellers *keep* the knife, why give it? Them fellers have gone away from here now.'"

Dionino did not come to see us, in fact, rather markedly, had not been near us since the scares started. He sent his good wishes one day via Sam who commented acidly, "Good wishes not much use to you fellers." Dionino, we gathered, had disgraced himself by making friends with the *carabiniere* corporal, indeed had possibly done worse. Sam had seen him driving round in a German truck—ostensibly in search of Antonio's wallet.

A visitor of another kind appeared through the scrub at the cave mouth unexpectedly, having climbed up from the valley. An uncouth Yugoslav soldier, as surprised to see us as we him. Mark, with his flair for nicknames, called him Caliban. He spoke a few words of Italian, a few of English, so communication was limited, but he had been with the Yugoslav detachment in the Sulmona barracks, had somehow escaped from the train near Popoli and, after walking south, had been living for a fortnight on a farm below Adullam, with a couple called Francesco and Margaretta. He was an unashamedly lazy creature and came up to the cave, he said, whenever Francesco suggested he should help with the work. Curiously, he recognized Mark, whom, so far as we could make out, he had seen several times in their compound.

Mark was rather evasive. "I suppose I called in there when I was trying to organize the place a bit."

But Caliban tried to convey something else. "You talk with big man. Englishman. Dark, like me." He made a gesture to indicate a garment worn round the neck.

"He means Kempster's *shech*," I said. "He's saying you talked to Kempster. Did you?"

"Not that I can remember," said Mark irritably.

To our annoyance Caliban asked us for food—we had little enough to spare and by no means shared Antonio's primeval attitude of hospitality towards strangers! However we gave him one of Lorenzo's apples—one that we had set aside as being unfit for human consumption, except in desperation. He ate it gratefully, core and all.

The next morning he reappeared. "It's always a mistake to encourage the lower classes," said Mark. But Caliban had brought a present of three baked potatoes. In return we gave him another rotten apple and, his gratitude overflowing, he began again to try to tell us something about Kempster, though we could hardly follow a word. There had been a German with them in the barracks, or Kempster himself had been a German—it was not clear which was meant. Then the station—that was easily understood. Kempster's *shech* came into it again, somehow. He had taken off his *shech*; at least Caliban, before leaving us for good, went through the motions of removing an imaginary scarf from his neck and putting it round Mark's, to the latter's disgust.

"It was only his way of showing his affection for Prospero," said Amos. "To him you were some kind of a god, I expect."

Mark told us a little more of his own background. The Belfast whelk-monger had made enough money to send his son, Mark's father, to Oxford. The son turned out brilliantly, married and settled down as a divinity don. Mark's mother died soon after the birth of his younger sister. The divinity don disliked and ignored his daughter but concentrated his affections on the boy, reading him the Greek New Testament at an age when *The Tale of the Flopsy Bunnies* would have been more appropriate. Mark had won a scholarship to Winchester, another back to Oxford—where he had remained till the war.

"I'm afraid it broke my father's heart when I read history instead of Greats. At any rate he died when I was an undergraduate. I can't pretend I've led a very full life. In a funny sort of way, I'm not sure I haven't enjoyed the last three weeks more than the rest put together."

On our sixth day in Adullam, towards evening, someone approached by the track, whistling "The British Grenadiers."

"Frank, how are you? We were getting worried."

He apologized for his long neglect of us (as it seemed) but explained that the Germans had occupied the building next door and that he too had been hiding in a cave. He was suffering from rheumatism in consequence. He was also suffering, still more acutely if less consciously, from a sense of persecution by his antipathetic brother-in-law, who, he was sure, had been trying to betray him to the Germans. "But they know I am armed. So far—God save the King—they've kept out of my path."

He had with him a letter, written in English, that Marshall and Snelgrove had sent by a messenger to their friends in the village. The peasants had asked Frank to translate it. The generals and their batmen, we learnt, were now living up on the Maiella in a hut in the woods. They had been contacted there by two representatives of the Eighth Army, sent through the lines to help escaping P.O.W.s. The representatives told them that the Eighth Army had taken Isernia and hoped to be in Sulmona in a week or two. It was possible, but extremely difficult, to reach the lines in three days across the mountains and they strongly advised the generals to wait.

This was fascinating news—the nearest to the horse's mouth we were likely to get, and we thanked Frank warmly for coming with it. The next week or two, he thought, would be critical in the valley. The Germans would certainly seize whatever food they could before withdrawing, ransack every farm, and behave altogether with calculated "frightfulness."

We could do nothing to help Sam and Antonio through the approaching crisis. On the contrary, our presence in the valley enormously complicated their lives and increased their dangers. The best course would be to get right out of the way and return to Little Ease, to wait there. We knew the path and Amos felt he could manage the climb if we took it slowly. Sam himself arrived while we were discussing the plan. He was always rather amused by Frank and trusted him absolutely, as we did. He agreed to bring us food before first light the next morning—as much as we could carry in the rucksack, which should last us a week. If the Allies came before that, he'd fetch us at once. Frank talked of coming up there with us himself, but we persuaded him that life in Little Ease, even for so short a time, would make his rheumatism worse.

Sam parted from us first with the promise to be back as arranged before dawn. Frank followed, calling out gaily that we would hoist a Union Jack on Sulmona's highest campanile when the day came. His spirit was indeed indomitable and we could hear the strains of "The British Grenadiers" for several minutes after he had vanished.

It was many weeks before we saw him again.

Manfredo in 1963

Antonio Crugnale and his wife in 1963

Sinibaldo Amatangelo in 1963

CHAPTER XIV

"So Mark had an affair with Kempster's sister at the end of the war. How strange . . ."

I'd come back to the table, more amused now by this ancient scrap of gossip than by chasing after a hypothetical Croce who would have vanished into the crowd at the fair.

"Why shouldn't he have done?" Matthew smiled, pleased with the success of his little ruse to avoid being left alone.

"No reason at all, really. Except—well, I'd always imagined he was the other way inclined."

"Oh. Did he give you some trouble?"

"Not of that sort. But something he once said. Anyway, who cares? What did she tell you about him?"

"Nothing particular. Sent her love when I next saw him."

"How did they meet?"

"She and her mother were stuck in Florence through the war. They had a rabbit-warren of a house in a quiet little piazza . . ."

"The Piazza San Martino di Parma . . ."

"So you know it?"

"No. But the name rings a distant bell. And Mark turned up on his ancient monuments racket?"

"Yes, soon after the Liberation. She'd been out of touch with Henry for years—and was desperately worried about him, of course. Mark, I gather, had been a great friend of his—with him in a prison camp—or something . . ."

"And could tell her he was dead . . . Well, I get the picture. She was emotionally grateful for the news. To him it counted as salvaging works of art . . ."

"Don't be so cynical." Matthew sounded quite annoyed. "She'd been through a ghastly time—hiding Jewish refugees and escaped prisoners in the cellars, running every kind of risk." Matthew recovered his temper and laughed. "Anyway, I don't suppose her brother came into it. Zozo just took a passing fancy to old Mark. She's the least inhibited person I know and suffers from guilt even less than I do!"

"Zozo?"

"A childhood nickname but she's never called anything else. Of course she's much younger than me, but I've known her most of my life."

"I thought I heard her introduced as *Contessa* something."

"Duodena. Count Duodena was hell, from what I hear. She pushed him off years ago."

"She's not re-married?"

"Not at present. Marriage interferes with her travels. She's done some remarkable trips—for a woman, that is. Actually I ran across her in Persia this time. As a rule she lets the house in the Piazza San Martino but she's back now for a few weeks. You'd like her—at least I *think* so. I must introduce you."

"Sometime. Brilliant personalities scare the pants off me. Well, I must push along to my peasants . . ."

"Why not have another drink, first? I can't believe you're as frantic to see them as all that."

"A quick one, perhaps." I signaled to the waiter and sat down again. "To be honest, I rather dread seeing them."

"It's always a mistake to go back. I never do."

"That's because you're romantic about the simple way of life. You like to preserve an illusion. I have no illusions. And to go back is really all one can do to show one's gratitude—to show one *cares*. I do care. I loved the old pattern but I also want it to change—for the better. I want my friends to have an easier time of it than they had."

"It won't make them happier. In fact, less happy."

"Who's cynical now? And it's not a question of *riches*." I broke off as the waiter brought the drinks. "Look," I said, when we were settled. "I'm no economist, and you've lived with many primitive peoples so you probably know more about this than I do. But surely Man's first aim, after food and warmth, is to have a surplus, to produce enough to *sell*? Civilization only starts from there—or so one was taught at school."

"Yes, I would agree. A trading surplus—of grain, or skins, or camels, or women. Not necessarily cash."

"Well, cash is what counts in the Abruzzi—and most places. My friends were living on no margin at all; at any time, though the war made it worse. Sam had *no* money, Antonio only a little—and he lost most of that on one memorable occasion, because of us. Amos once said, jokingly, that he hoped they regarded us as an investment. I'm quite certain they didn't.

"They were totally simple people, on the brink of starvation. They knew nothing about the reasons for the war. It was just a great impersonal sort of disaster—the fault of the Government. So far as they were concerned we were three strangers whom it had thrown on to them. And we were even poorer than themselves. In fact destitute. So they helped us. Just that. The thought of repayment afterwards never entered their heads—there was little certainty that the war would finish and no probability at all that we'd be able to repay them. Of course they were glad enough of such money as they got in the end. I sent all I could. So did Mark, I believe. And being in Italy he was able to screw some more out of Military Government. When I last saw them they seemed to think they'd been *generously* treated; at least they were a little better off financially, or that was my impression."

The second *campari* loosened my tongue and I went on about it longer than I meant. "What they'd done could hardly be counted in money . . . Things became impossible in the valley. We went and lived up in a cave, expecting to be there a week. Actually the Germans had dug in to their famous *Winterstellung* and the line remained static for months. We had to stay in the cave. Sam and Antonio climbed up there every four or five days with food. Up and back. Six or seven hours, on top of their farmwork, on top of the rest of the worry. For the last three weeks they did it under snow. Sam even carried an iron shoemakers-last up on his back once—to mend my boots. Two simple peasants. And they'd never heard of us till a

week before. We belonged to a different race, an invading army—
but you'll get more of an idea when we've been up that mountain tomorrow—if we succeed in getting up it. I'm not sure I shall. That's
one thing, perhaps, that I've come to find out. I'm about the same
age now as they were then."

"How far is it?"

"Three to four hours, if we keep going."

"That's not much. I walked a thousand miles last month at ten
hours a day over damn' sight larger mountains than that . . ."

"Yes, yes. You're extremely fit and tough. And you were doing it
for pleasure. Sam and Antonio certainly weren't. Nor did they *have*
to do it. But it wasn't just the guts, or the sacrifice. It's—something
else, though God knows what, that's so important, I feel. One was a
bronze-age Pelignus, more or less. Deep in his heart he still believed
in the magic power of snakes—and I wouldn't say he was wrong.
The other was, if not an atheist, certainly not a do-gooding Christian. He loathed established religion. He was, in his own way, as
much a skeptic as Mark and Amos, though he believed in a Deity
of some kind, a sort of abstract principle of what was, and was *not*,
right. But no reward in Heaven, nothing like that. And meanwhile
a damned unpleasant sort of reward on earth, if he wasn't careful."

There's a glazed look that comes down on my friends' faces,
as impenetrable as a safety curtain, when I start talking about my
Abruzzi peasants. I know the look. It grieves me. But, once started,
I am hardly more unable to stop than a Royal Mail express train;
come to think of it, I am less able to stop.

"When did you last see them?" said Matthew, glazing.

"The first time was in August 1947. Lucinda and I caught a
train from Rome to Popoli and then a bus. Sam's eldest son had
just died—pneumonia, the result mostly of undernourishment in
the war. They were marvelously the same. They gave us an overwhelming welcome. But the heat was stifling. We had splitting
headaches—and we had to drink with everyone, to do justice to one
meal after another. Six heavy peasant meals between midday and
midnight. Then we slept in Sam's best bed—we were eaten alive.
We slunk away next morning. Sam and Antonio saw us off from
Pettorano Station. "You won't come back again," they said. "What is

there for people like you in this sort of place? We only stay here because we have to!"

"But you went back?" The safety curtain was about half-way down.

"A few years later. Passing through somewhere. By then Sam had
left for the States with both remaining sons. His wife was running
the farm single-handed. Antonio was O.K.—he had a lorry which
he hired out. But his wife and Sam's had quarreled. They were very
different types. It was all rather embarrassing and painful."

"And now Sam is back from the States?" The curtain was almost
down.

"Yes. He wrote to me in Florence. He was there a dozen years.
Just working as a roadmender—he was run over by a car and badly
injured at one stage. But he saved enough money for the fare, with
some over, I hope. The sons have stopped in the States. Fully qualified Americans—and married to girls from this valley whom they
met out there. He sent me the wedding photos. Large fat young men
in dinner jackets with button holes. Of course, they've done the best
thing . . ."

"Ah well," said Matthew. "*Eheu fugaces . . .* Let's have another
drink and I'll tell you about my meeting with Zozo in Persian Kurdistan."

"Later," I said, getting up. "This time I really am off. Don't forget your call to Florence. See you at dinner."

Sam wouldn't have changed, I knew. Not, that is, in anything
that mattered. But I had changed. And that was what troubled me.

"Supposing," said Amos, whittling away with *il pastore's* knife. "Supposing you could strip away civilization, layer upon layer, as I'm
doing with this stick. Strip away the conventions, the inherited re-
flexes, the religious beliefs and attitudes, all the accumulated para-
phernalia of accepted behaviour and custom, and get down to the
irreducible minimum, to the small but enormous step that divides
the savage from what we are pleased to think of as a civilized man.
What would you have?"

Mark thought about it—time was no object—while he cleared a
space in the fire, in order to bake a potato. "You're not talking about
the soul, I take it?"

"Lord, no. Savages have souls, one is told."

"I don't know that I can put it in one word. But the ability to use the brain clearly and constructively. To *concentrate*." Mark concentrated his brain for a minute on the baking of the potato. "The power to absorb knowledge, to become educated. Something of that sort, at any rate."

"Something less intellectual, more instinctive than that," I said. "Stupid people are often more civilized than clever ones—that is if I understand Amos's point rightly. Something to do with imagination, with being able to see yourself in perspective and therefore being able to *anticipate*. I'm evolving a theory. If we stop up here another six months I may have worked it out in greater detail."

"God forbid," said Mark. "This potato will need five more minutes. And what's *your* irreducible minimum?"

"Oh, nothing as complicated as any of that." Amos examined the piece of wood, now matchstick thin, testing its point. He was trying to make a bodkin, with which to mend a rent in his bush-shirt. "As a child I was taken once to see the source of a great river—the Rhine or the Rhone, or was it the Thames?—anyway, I remember there was a tiny spring bubbling up from the ground. I was staggered to think that the enormous river started from a bit of water you could block up with your hat. I believe that the whole of civilization comes down, simply, to disinterested *kindness*. I don't mean kindness between children and parents—that's basic. But kindness to strangers, to men in general. The rest follows from that—as the river grows from the spring."

He glanced at the little valley below us, to where a spiral of smoke curled up through a thick clump of beeches. The leaves had not yet fallen and nothing was visible in the clump except the movement of a cow whisking its tail against the flies. A family of peasants from Pettorano, two *giovanotti* and their father, were camping in a hut made of branches. They had brought their cow up the mountain for safety and we'd found them already there when we arrived at Little Ease from Adullam a fortnight earlier.

"I only thought of it," said Amos, "because, when we've eaten that potato, we've nothing left except two elderly apples. Micky and Minnie pinched the last walnut in the night. Sam and Antonio won't be here till the day after tomorrow. So our only hope depends, once again, on our friends in the hut being—civilized. They're cooking something now, by the look of it."

The girls of the Pettorano family made the three-hour climb with food for their men each day. They turned up punctually every morning at nine o'clock whatever the weather, barefoot and singing, with a laden donkey and further dishes on their heads, and even maintained that they enjoyed the exercise. Occasionally one of them would climb the farther distance up to us with an offering, for which we were thankful indeed.

Sam or Antonio or both, accompanied usually by one or other of their children, visited us about every fourth day with as much as they could spare, or carry—huge loaves of bread, pieces of veal or pork (they killed their pigs to ensure the Germans wouldn't get them), a cheese or a pot of honey, and sometimes scraps of chicken, the bones of which we would use to flavor a broth for weeks. (We'd brought a billycan this time.) Walnuts, almonds, and apples completed the diet, and we thrived on it. But the mountain air, the daily walk to the *fontana*, and the search for fuel, made us damnably hungry, the supplies never quite lasted out, even with strict rationing, and we were seldom without a gnawing pain in our bellies.

Our economy was rigid to the point of absurdity, every morsel being divided scrupulously into three. The quinine pills were long since finished. Amos's bouts of malaria recurred every two or three days. The slightest effort brought on a shivering fit, when Mark and I had to add the warmth of our bodies to the cloaks and blanket before he recovered. Unable to leave the cave he was cook and storeman, while Mark and I fetched wood and water. We became steadily grimier. Our hair grew into birds' nests, our beards daily more impressive—nowadays the sight of a beatnik moves me with nostalgia. We even had two pet mice, Micky and Minnie, who stole our crumbs cautiously at first, then with increasing boldness, till they took no notice of us whatever. It must have been the most prosperous period of their lives.

On the way up from Adullam to Little Ease we had stopped to watch a flight of Spitfires machine-gunning the Strada Nazionale. Since then we had seen Allied planes two or three times and heard the faintest rumble of gunfire. Otherwise we lived in a vacuum, so far as the war went, apart from the odd rumor of its progress relayed by Sam and Antonio or the Pettorano girls. Isernia, we gathered, had still not fallen and as the weeks passed we realized, with increasing dismay and bitterness, that the two representatives of the Eighth Army had given Marshall and Snelgrove a wildly over-optimistic picture of the situation.

Now and then Sam brought a scribbled message from Frank. His health was bad, he had had to leave his cave and was living again with his sister in spite of the continual menace of his *carabiniere* brother-in-law whose character became ever more uncongenial. But he always ended on a note of unshakable patriotism and patient courage in the face of his many trials. "God save the King! Rule Britannia! Your humble servant, Frank Del Signore." Once he sent us a present of tobacco, which started a craze for cutting ourselves pipes from beech-roots. The tobacco finished, we smoked crumbled leaves—without the smallest pleasure, even with the liberal aid of imagination. *Il pastore*'s knife was a priceless treasure, needing to be shared as jealously as the food. When I had my turns, I gradually carved a portrait of my wife on a chunk of beechwood, handing it eventually for safe keeping to Sam. In 1947 he handed it back to me from its storage place in the family wedding-chest, a strange totemistic object that now stares at me from the table where I write.

At such close range, there was not much that Amos, Mark, and I didn't know of one another's characters. I'd said nothing to Mark of what *il professore* had told me, and as I came to understand him better, and to like him far better too, the idea of him having in some manner betrayed *il professore* to Croce seemed more and more improbable. I could imagine him mixed up in any sort of Machiavellian intrigue—such as we had seen at Athlit. But there was nothing in the least mean in his nature, indeed he exacted from himself standards of honesty compared with which Amos and I were common crooks. Still, something rather odd must have occurred in Vasco and I waited for an opportunity to have it out with him in private.

For the first few days two British sergeants were living with the Pettorano family in their hut. At the Armistice they had escaped from the Sulmona barracks on to the Maiella with the rest, but had been driven down again when the Germans seized the main water points. Reaching Pettorano they were adopted by this family and came up with the men to the woods. They believed that the British had reached the Sangro and set off to walk there by the route over Genzana that I had seen from the *fontana* with Dionino. They returned defeated the next evening. There was, they said, a big gorge to be crossed, in which the Germans had a petrol dump and troops high up in the woods. Their verdict was that the route was impossible, and they left us, this time to try walking towards the lines down the valleys. Once again we exchanged names—and long afterwards I heard that they got through in the end.

We suspected that the difficulty was not so great as they claimed, particularly as they admitted that the gorge could be skirted at its top if you were prepared "to go mountaineering." We debated whether to make the attempt ourselves before the snows came, after which Amos's and Mark's footwear would rule it out, always supposing that Amos himself had enough strength to walk the distance at all. In early November Mark and I decided to make a long reconnaisance.

It was a clear day, with an icy wind that foreboded snow—and in fact the snow came, a great quantity of it, the day after. Leaving Amos wrapped up warmly by the fire, we climbed through the woods to the first *fontana*, then along the spine of Genzana. We passed two more *fontane* and after three hours came to a fourth, where we found some boys watering a small flock of sheep. Their home was in Rocca Pia, far down to the east of us, on the edge of the famous Plain of Cinquemiglia where we could see the glint of German vehicles and where, Mark said, an army had once perished in snowdrifts. Climbing the peak of Genzana we looked beyond Monte Rotella to the east as far as the Adriatic horizon; in the opposite direction down on to Scanno and its lake and, behind that, to the more wooded mountains that contained the National Park with its bears and wolves. Directly to our south Genzana merged into a farther range, that ended with Monte Greco above the Sangro— a dozen-odd miles away, and we identified the gorge mentioned by the sergeants, to avoid which we would need to go "mountaineering."

From the map, there would be about the same distance to cover between the Sangro and Isernia. On my own I should be able to do it easily, I thought. Neither of the others had the same determination, nor the same incentive, to reach home. For a minute I was tempted to set off there and then. And it would be one less mouth to feed. "Well, goodbye, Mark," I would say. "See you in Oxford some day, maybe." Perhaps I would have gone. I don't know. But he said quietly, "If Amos wasn't in that cave, I think, having come this far, you and I could do it, couldn't we? Well, we'd better be getting back to the old boy, or he'll wonder what the devil's happened."

Snow-clouds were massing up behind the Sasso and the Maiella. We might have been a couple of friends on a walking tour, rather than two fugitives temporarily suspended above an abysmal future. We'd brought a crust of bread and lay down in a sheltered spot, to eat it and rest, before returning. Then I repeated to Mark exactly what *il professore* had told me about him.

He listened calmly, and with a faint smile. "So my crimes have caught up with me," he said. "Vasco . . . What a long time ago that already seems . . . Yes, I did tell Croce. But not perhaps for the reason you think. It was hard to know what else to do." Mark munched a piece of crust before continuing. "You see, the Germans were watching the camp—and all the other camps—like hawks, long before the Armistice. Simply as a security precaution. The Italian Commandant was in terror of them. Of course they'd got hold of Croce early on. Croce, who really ran the camp, was playing a double game, waiting to see which way the war went and trying to keep in both with the S.B.O. and Germans."

"*Il professore* was already working for you?"

"More or less. He was pro-British, but really he also was waiting to see how things turned out. You can't blame him. He was scared of Croce and Croce mistrusted him. Each knew too much about the other, I suppose. Anyway, of the two I got on better with Croce. Perhaps, being Irish, I could understand him. He was a proud man, something of a patriot. He wanted to do whatever seemed best for his own country. When the Allies landed at Salerno he reckoned the time had come to side with us. He and I agreed that if there was an Armistice or something of that kind—a tricky period between the Italians laying down their arms and the arrival of the British—it was essential to keep people from wandering off in their hundreds. That would be inviting the Germans to step in—and might end in a tragedy. The S.B.O. agreed. Croce undertook to keep the Germans off—so long as we stayed. The Germans damned nearly took over the camp on 3rd September I believe, as they grabbed others farther north. However, thanks largely to Croce, they didn't."

"What about the famous War Office order? Was that faked?"

Mark laughed. "Not entirely. There *was* an order—to all camps. We gave it a more personal touch, perhaps. But that came later, so far as I remember." He sighed. "How involved it all is. To complicate it further, there was this idea of blowing the Pescara bridge . . ."

"Ah," I said.

"I'd hatched the idea a month before. It was only an *idea*—and not such a bad one. The S.B.O. and his Adjutant took it up rather more than I intended. When that bombing raid happened they decided to carry the plan out—as you know. But they never told *me*. I'm afraid they were rather jealous of me—if that doesn't sound too immodest. But regular soldiers have a complex about amateur intelligence officers. They were glad to use me—but had to show their independence. Anyway I only heard of it quite by chance a day or two before it was due to take place. Kempster told me, actually. I was appalled—it was just the sort of excuse the Germans were waiting for. I tried to dissuade them—and was told to mind my own business. So I stopped it the only way I could—by tipping off Croce. Was I wrong?"

"Quite right," I said. "So far as I'm concerned! Did you know Kempster was coming with us?"

"Poor Kempster. Yes. He consulted me about maps. I knew him quite well at Athlit, though I never cared much for him at that time. Too aggressive and—well, Germanic. Though he was brought up in England and a bitter anti-Nazi, his father was German and German Intelligence had its eye on him. You'd think they had bigger things to worry about than catching small fish like Kempster but the Nazis have a particularly vindictive hate of lapsed nationals, or, as I suppose they look at it, traitors. By ill chance, when he was caught in Sardinia, the German H.Q. got his name . . ."

"He was betrayed by a guide sent from Algiers . . ."

"No, it wasn't that, I gather. Apparently an officer spoke in German to a sentry on an airfield, before the planes were sabotaged . . ."

"But that was *me*! I quoted something of Schiller's, to try to pass myself off as a German-speaking Italian."

"Well, for some reason or other it made them wild and they got hold of the list of officers from the Italians. By then you'd all been sent to Vasco. After another time-lag, German H.Q. at L'Aquila were told to try to get him—which is the stage I came into it. By then we'd been moved to Sulmona. The Commandant asked me if there was an officer called Kempster in the camp. I had the sense to guess what it was all about and said I was sure there wasn't. But I tipped Kempster off—he joined the Yugoslavs. The Germans had a chap in there already, I believe. I'm afraid he spotted Kempster— at least that's my guess. That scarf thing he wore made him conspicuous. I suppose the sentry was told to shoot him boarding the train on the slightest excuse. And did. Well, come on. Amos will be worrying . . ."

For such an upright man, Mark was a good liar.

CHAPTER XV

When Mark and I rejoined Amos, he told us that the family from Pettorano had decamped. They knew that the snow was coming and their girls would no longer be able to carry up food.

It snowed hard for a couple of days. At least we were saved climbing to the *fontana*—we simply stuffed snow into the water-bottle and melted it over the fire. The family had left plenty of logs behind too, which I fetched. We built a barricade of branches against the cave mouth and settled down quite comfortably, unless it thawed when every inch of the cave's roof steadily dripped.

Sam and Antonio came as before, every third or fourth day. The snow added an hour on to their journey each way. They thought we were mad, preferring to remain rather than go back with them—as they urged us to. At heart, I think, they were thankful when we declined. But could they go on bringing up food? Oh yes, of course they could. It was nothing. They used the long hard route, rather than be seen by people in Pettorano. Sometimes they were a day late—and we could have wept with relief when we heard them shout a greeting as they crossed the shaly slope. The Germans hadn't raided their own farms yet, but most of the rest. We could assess the state of nerves in the valley by whether Sam referred to the Ger-

mans as "them Germany peoples" or as "them Germany bastards."
If they had done something particularly outrageous they became
"them Germany sons-of-bitches." But most of his indignation was
reserved for us—and the mess we were in.

"That's not *right*, you fellers living like that!"

The fact that his cap, coat, and knee-breeches, indeed his very
skin, were wringing wet as a rule, did not trouble him at all—
though the temperature was at freezing-point. As for Antonio, who
seldom wore even a coat, he would point to the bare chest under the
cotton shirt and chuckle. Whichever daughter had come, carrying
the hot dish in its napkin on her head and still dressed merely in a
shift, would often be blue in the face, her teeth chattering noisily.
From time to time we gave each man another "cheque"—against
the Allied arrival—in case something happened to us in the mean-
time. They pocketed the scraps of paper, more from politeness than
because they thought the paper meant anything.

The fire became an Olympic flame, a god—and we its priests.

People say that it's only the experiences of childhood that last
through one's life and certainly the very old seem able to recall their
extreme youth with undiminished clarity. Perhaps, in my old age,
a door at present closed will softly open. But for the past twenty
years the experience that is most habitually and vividly conjured
up by a chance smell or taste—my little madeleine, so to speak—
is of that cave in the Abruzzi. This is not nostalgia for the war, or
even for my youth. I can bathe in a sandy cove in the sun without
being reminded of Athlit. A bottle of Palestine hock would evoke no
memory of the pirate camp and a soup of disgusting weeds would
mean nothing to me—except a stomach ache. But a wood fire, any
wood fire, anywhere . . . As soon as I see one I am impelled to keep
it alight, to worry that the supply of fuel is running out. And, standing by one, even in my own house, I think—I always think—of
Amos and of Mark.

We learnt all the poetry that Mark could remember; we played
ridiculous memory games; we invented the titles of unlikely
books—*Cattle Stealing in the West* by Bertrand Russell, *All Passion
Spent* by Kraft Ebbing, *Where Engels Fears to Tread* by Kant; we
argued whether it is better to have a good picture by a bad artist or
a bad picture by a good artist; we exchanged imaginary dreams . . .

"I dreamt," I said, "of a small Georgian house with a lot of out-buildings and a few acres of rough garden and orchard. I was standing with my wife and son admiring a Jersey cow and a fresh litter of pigs . . ."

"I was in the Bodleian," said Mark. "I had all day in front of me and I had sent for the 5 volumes of Howarth's *History of the Mongols* . . ."

"I was sitting in a little café off the Boulevard St. Germain," said Amos. "I'd ordered two brioches and a café au lait . . ."

Once Mark tripped over a pile of logs on the ledge outside and fell most of the way down the slope in the slush. He returned to dry by the fire in a mood that was, to say the least, anti-social. Amos said, "There's a basic satisfaction in slapstick humor that nothing else quite gives. I have a friend called Lord Furlo—this is a true story, I was with him in New York. He's a mild sort of chap but much tougher than he looks—he got a boxing blue. A cop stopped us for some reason I forget in a little street off Broadway and asked our names. When Furlo gave his the cop simply knocked him down, like that. Furlo stood up and said, 'Why did you do that?' The cop said, 'Sorry pal, but I've never hit an English lord before.' My friend said quietly, 'Perhaps you were never hit by one either.' He knocked the cop out cold and we walked away rather quickly."

We talked of Socialism, of Lloyd George, of the Battle of Ala-mein, of the Thirty-Nine Articles, of the Marx Brothers, of John Betjeman's poetry. We talked, a little, of sex. Mark told us of *Fanny Hill* which he had read and we had never heard of. "Oh, you have a great treat in store. Delicious stuff, beautifully written and some-how innocently frank. Straight sex—that's why it's banned, one pre-sumes. It says that love is natural and fun."

"In the end it becomes a bore," said Amos. "If you consider it, there isn't enough variety. Only about four positions possible to any-one less than a trained contortionist. Back—front—vertical—hor-izontal. Oh, a few mutations. Whereas I can think of thirty-seven absolutely different varieties of cheese, I was counting them up last night. I wish we had even one of them here at this minute, but I'm damned if I feel like making love."

"I'm a Celt," said Mark. "I am interested in spiritual matters— and sex is nothing if not a spiritual matter. The real preoccupation of the Anglo-Saxon race is not with sex, but with status, with class. Anglo-Saxons are specialists in minute social distinctions, at judging strangers by their ties and shoes and accent. If an English couple is sitting in a foreign restaurant and another English couple comes in, each whispers together, eyeing the other. What are they whispering? Not 'I wonder if they're lovers, or married, or impotent.' But 'I guess a schoolmaster.' 'No, too well-dressed. A dentist.' 'She's obviously married beneath her,' and so on. Unlike us Celts, at heart Anglo-Saxons are without passion. Perhaps that is why they are so civilized . . ."

"Rubbish," I interrupted. "We are tremendously passionate, under the reserve. You have only to consider our poetry. We're civilized because we realize that the whole of civilization depends on someone being prepared to give way. That's why we don't mind being beaten by Australia at cricket. The civilized man *prefers* to lose . . ."

"Heaven knows what you're both talking about," said Amos. "But thank God for uncivilized men who are willing to climb for four hours up a mountain and back in order to feed three worthless strangers. If I was the Almighty, and if mankind could only produce us, I'd scrap it. Because it can produce Sam and Antonio, I'd give it another chance. Which reminds me, I'm bloody hungry, aren't you? I hope to God they turn up!"

They did turn up.

The intermittent thaws stopped, the cave roof ceased to drip, the snow crystallized on the bare beeches, the thick tonsure was reduced to a transparent stubble on the mountain's contours. The little valley was *ours*. We felt like the last survivors of the human race. And we were as much irritated as curious when, on the last day of November, a large party of men and donkeys emerged out of the gorge from Pettorano.

"Bloody trespassers," said Amos.

Most of them halted below, at the hut in the beech clump. Two, incoherent with excitement, scrambled on up to us. The Germans had announced they were about to move the entire population of Pettorano to North Italy for labor, separating men and women into different camps near Padua. Most of the village was therefore fleeing up the mountain with their livestock and all the possessions they could carry. This was the advance guard, come to build huts and prepare for the rest. The two men asked to share Little Ease. It was, they said, not for themselves, who could support sleeping in the open, but for their women and *bambini*. In all they were a family of eleven. If we agreed, they would enlarge the cave at once and construct a shelter in front.

We could scarcely refuse, for Little Ease was the only cave on the mountain at this level, and moreover, if Sam and Antonio were in the same desperate straits, we might have to depend on these people for food. So we agreed. It did not occur to us, till too late, that our friends might themselves be wishing to come and share the cave. They were not due to visit us for another two days.

One of the men was young, small, and wiry, with dynamic energy and a vicious temper. He suffered from malaria and his face was primrose-colored. Mark called him Yellow Peril. The other, his father, was elderly and slightly mad. We called him Old Misery. Yellow Peril began work at once with pick and shovel, deepening and widening the cave, building a platform out from its mouth on which to support the shelter. He felled trees, hurled rocks about, hammered branches into position with a demonic rage, swearing at Old Misery who pottered about in the background. We squatted in the snow to one side, indignant at the intrusion, anxious for the future, and wondering guiltily whether we should have kept the cave free for Sam and Antonio in case they were counting on it. In fact, if we had tried to keep it, Yellow Peril would probably have battered us with his pick-axe, for the strength and fury of his tiny body were elemental.

In the afternoon Sam and Antonio suddenly appeared. They had not yet had orders to move but were expecting them hourly and so had brought us fresh supplies, in case. For once they looked tired and worried. We could not tell whether they had wanted to use Little Ease or discover what plans they were making to protect their families and cattle. They brushed aside our fears that we had let them down, urging us not to bother about *them*. Instead they were indignant with Yellow Peril and Old Misery for disturbing us and, so far as we could follow the conversation, told them bluntly that we must be allowed to stay in the cave whatever happened. They departed, with the promise to come back in a few days. That, in such circumstances, they should have found time to think of us at all, let alone spend six or seven hours climbing to see if we were all right, left us staring after them in silence for many minutes, unable to find words.

At least, we thought, the German action might be an omen that the battle was approaching. Sam believed the Allies had reached Castel di Sangro. For some nights we had seen gun flashes behind the Maiella, and it needed little military instinct to guess that the Eighth Army was pushing up the coast, in order to outflank the Germans' position in the center. However the trains still rattled across Rotella. The viaducts were all said to be mined and we should hear their explosion long before British troops reached the Gizio Valley.

By evening the work was done. Yellow Peril and Old Misery descended to Pettorano to fetch the rest of the family. In the night a wind blew up and by morning it was deluging rain and sleet. Little Ease dripped as never before and water poured through the roof of the rough shelter. Several families began to arrive in the valley. Ours ascended the hillside towards us, their donkeys and ponies laden with bedding, sacks of corn, cooking pots, everything movable.

There were five women, the eldest eighty, all with blankets over their heads on which they carried further stores, and dragging four sodden children. At first they were astonishingly cheerful, chattering and laughing as they built up the fire, unpacked and generally moved in to a home they had not dreamt of occupying two days earlier. Yellow Peril was having a bad malarial attack. Shivering and sweating, he unloaded the animals and tethered them among the trees while he cursed Mussolini, Old Misery, the Germans, the whole of existence—and his womenfolk. They bore it patiently for a few hours, then broke down, and the next days stay clearly in my mind for the continuous sound of wailing—sometimes shrieking, when Yellow Peril beat his wife with a shovel. At night all fourteen of us somehow piled on top of one another and the stores were stacked round the sides. They had brought plenty of meal and potatoes, a cow which they tied up nearby, and even some chickens for which they scooped a hollow in the cave floor. We shared their polenta—maize flour boiled into a thick paste—and some delicious baked quinces. The fire, kept going on the platform, poured smoke into the cave incessantly and Amos developed a painful inflammation of the eyes. The women's incompetence at stoking the fire became the cause of innumerable further squabbles between them and Yellow Peril. They smacked the children, the children fought one another, the horror of the whole thing is indescribable.

The grandmother, whose name was Maddalena, huddled over the fire, cooking up dishes of beans or chillis for Old Misery who spent his time otherwise leading the animals to water at the *fontana*. He seemed always to be wetter than anyone else and rarely spoke, so plunged was he in gloom. They were a fine-looking couple, with the special dignity that only old peasants possess, and we felt deeply for them. On the third afternoon, as we sat talking to Maddalena, she questioned us about ourselves. How did three Englishmen come to be living in the cave? When had we escaped? Who had been looking after us all this time?

Why, Sinibaldo and Antonio, we said. They had been up the day she arrived surely—but no, the day before. We poured out a little of what was in our hearts. Did she know them?

Oh yes, everyone in the valley knew everyone. They were good men—but no better than many others. The times were cruel. She and her husband had worked hard all their lives. They had always been to church, believed in God and the Madonna, observed the Feasts of the Saints. And now this. Why? What had they done to be thus treated at the end of their lives? The Germans had ransacked their house even of its doors and windows. Except for some stores left buried, all their life's belongings were now with them in this cave. We tried to say something of comfort, but there was nothing that could honestly be said, to mitigate her utter despair. One of the younger women, standing against the shelter's entrance, whispered "*Tedeschi!*" Two German soldiers with rifles were five yards off.

Mark, Amos, and I plunged under the bedding at the back of the cave. The rest, with great presence of mind, stood up and crowded the entrance. We covered ourselves over as best we could in a matter of seconds. Peeping out I could see two pairs of gaitered legs and the young face of one of the soldiers. They were part of a patrol, come to collect the cattle hidden on the mountain, and after a hurried conversation Yellow Peril and Old Misery accompanied them to the cow. When they had gone, the women implored us hysterically to leave at once or they would all be shot. Grabbing our cloaks we scampered up the hillside in the other direction and squatted down out of sight in the snow. Later Yellow Peril brought up the rucksack and water-bottle. He was almost speechless with fright, rage, malaria. The Germans had taken the cow. They had also told him that the English were at Pescara. "Go and join your own people," he jabbered. "Go! Go! And don't come near *us*!"

We had no food. Amos's and Mark's feet were half-frozen. The best thing—the only thing—to be done was to return to the valley and throw ourselves on Sam's mercy, until we could find boots and walk. We were too cautious by now to believe the news that the English had reached Pescara. Still it bore out our theory that they were pushing up the coast, that the line was much closer. At nightfall we staggered wearily across the shale, over the grassy shoulder past the fig tree where the snowline ended, and along the track through the scrub near Adullam. We tapped softly on the shutters of Sam's kitchen at about 10 P.M. and he let us in.

Unbelievably enough he appeared delighted to see us. The Germans had taken Antonio's cow, but his was still hidden safely in the cave where he and Antonio looked after it in turns. Otherwise they had lost nothing and had not yet been threatened with transportation. Sam's wife fried us sausages and, after bedding us down in the hay, Sam rushed off to tell Antonio what he was pleased to call "the good news."

Our wanderings—at least Amos's and mine—had entered their final phase.

The problem was boots.

Amos's feet were enormous, sizes larger even than Antonio's. Mark's and mine would fit an average pair if such a thing could be found, but, with snow about to descend on the whole valley at any minute, boots could only be bought for hard cash—a lot of hard cash.

While Sam started discreet inquiries we inhabited various caves along the hillside, staying hidden by night as well as day and moving position every so often to prevent our presence becoming known. He was on tenterhooks lest word got round that he was feeding us. Fascist spies were everywhere, often pretending to be escaped prisoners in order to tempt generous peasants into disaster. There were many gruesome stories of betrayals, and executions. Sam shaved our beards and admonished us, more solemnly even than I admonish my daughters, never, *never* to talk to strange men.

Despite all precautions our return to the valley and our whereabouts could not be kept entirely secret. Friends from the past would reappear mysteriously to visit us at whichever cave we had changed to. Some, like Frank, we were delighted to see again. He was dressed in his immaculate plus-fours and trilby hat and boldly heralded his approach with "The British Grenadiers." The Germans, he told us, were billeted all over the valley and he spent his days in a cave, returning at night to Gabriele on whose farm he was now living. His sister had gone to Sulmona to have a baby. His brother-in-law was fully employed by the Germans and wore a special arm-band. Frank had plenty to say about *him*! He came accompanied by Dionino, who looked rather shame-faced at having neglected us—though we certainly did not blame him for that. No talk now of *Sempre scappare* . . . That particular lark had lost its appeal. We noticed that neither Frank nor he any longer carried weapons. The danger of being shot, if found in possession of them, was too great. We told Frank about the boots and he promised to see what he could do. We also warned him—to his immense gratification—that he looked conspicuously English in his present attire and would do better to dress as one of the peasants whom he so evidently despised. Indomitable as ever, he bade us goodbye with a flourish of patriotic sentiments and strode off down the hill in daylight whistling, with a complete disregard of the danger, his signature tune. We never saw him again.

Lorenzo the miller frightened us out of our skins by appearing unannounced at our cave mouth—indeed, we frightened him too, for he had no idea we were there. Snow had fallen in the night, he had noticed footprints, and was looking in out of curiosity. He promised to return with a meal, but we never saw him again either. Sam, when we mentioned it, reminded us that Lorenzo's wife was notoriously mean. He shook his head uneasily. It was the sort of chance contact that could compromise his own position, for word passed round the valley swiftly. That night *il pastore* also materialized quietly from nowhere, to ask for his knife back. "Baldo still feeding you?" he asked slyly. "Good lord, no," we said. "Haven't heard of him for weeks." *Il pastore* pocketed his knife, smiled, and slipped away. We changed caves next morning.

The war was hotting up, the situation in the valley gathering to a crisis. There was no bombing, but Spitfires rat-tat-tatted on the Strada Nazionale, ack-ack guns went into action after them. Once we heard continuous shell-fire from beyond Sulmona. It lasted a few minutes. At that point we were occupying a cave somewhere above Gabriele's farm. Peering out cautiously we could see shells bursting on the face of Morrone. The Germans were demolishing Holy Humphrey, as a reprisal for his having sheltered an escaped prisoner. Another time a muffled explosion came from one of the houses below us. People began to hurry towards the house from the fields, women screamed, and a platoon of Germans ran towards it down a track. We learnt the explanation later. The platoon, billeted on the farm, had left a grenade lying on a table. A boy of seven had picked it up and been blown to pieces. The incident increased a nightmarish sense of being trapped. The near-escape from the German soldiers at Little Ease had shaken our nerve, we longed to be off—to be climbing Genzana with our fate entirely in our own hands. Moreover the burden of caring for us had become intolerable for Sam and Antonio—though they gave no sign of flinching from it.

The B.B.C. reported Villetta Barrea and Alfedena as definitely in British hands. Amos's malaria had not recurred for a week. He was confident of being able to manage the two or three nights' march needed to get there. Mark and I were sure we could find the way to the fourth *fontana*, even under snow. From then on we would have to depend on a combination of luck, cunning, and endurance.

If only we could all get some *boots*.

Frank sent us a letter with Dionino, also a present of tinned meat and cigarettes. By then we were in yet another cave—our last—but Dionino had no difficulty in tracking us down. Frank wrote that he was confident the British would arrive in Sulmona by Christmas. He thought he had found a large enough pair of boots for Amos. If we were set on walking he would have liked to accompany us himself but his rheumatism had returned and he was living permanently indoors, expecting his brother-in-law to have him arrested at any minute. God save the King . . .

Dionino brought the boots a day or two later, on 13th December. Frank had paid a peasant for them in cash—a generous action indeed for he had virtually no money. For what it was worth we sent him a "cheque" drawn on the Eighth Army. The boots were considerably too small but Amos managed to get into them with bare feet.

It remained to find some for Mark and myself. Sam had offered hopes of two pairs but was dead against the whole idea of us walking at all. "Them fellow too sick," he said of Amos. When he visited us as usual on the 14th we began at once to question him about the boots but something, clearly, was very wrong. He was in a state quite unlike himself, a mixture of panic, despair, and anger—anger with *us*.

Why, he burst out, had we told old Maddalena up at Little Ease that he and Antonio had looked after us? She and the family had come down from the mountain, unable to stick it further. By chance Maddalena had met *il pastore* and repeated what we'd said to her. He had told Gabriele, perhaps maliciously—for he thought Sam had slighted him about the knife. Now the story was round the whole valley. Sam didn't care so much, but Antonio and his wife were furious with us. Never wanted to hear of us again . . .

Utterly wretched, we could only stammer that we had meant him and Antonio no harm. Indeed, the contrary . . . How *could* we have been so foolish? he repeated. Then, abruptly, he shrugged and laughed. "Well, can't be helped, I guess." We got back to the question of boots. Yes, he'd found a couple of pairs. He'd paid the man a sack of flour for them and would bring them the next evening at dusk, with food for the journey. Again he tried to dissuade us but, seeing we were determined, said "All right. Then I come with you fellers." We firmly declined. Sam had done enough. We could hardly bear to impose on him another twenty-four hours. In the end we agreed he should accompany us as far as the first *fontana*—that much he insisted.

We spent the day excitedly preparing, overjoyed at the prospect of liberation, and refusing to contemplate failure. Amos stamped about the cave to work his boots on to his feet. We felt like schoolboys the last night of a long term. "This time in three—or even two—days . . ."

At dusk Sam arrived, and with him, we were thankful to see, Antonio. He too intended to come as far as the *fontana*. They had brought so much food that we could barely get it into the rucksack. Nothing was said of Maddalena. We wanted to apologize to Antonio, to try to make things right. Yet, if we spoke, we were as likely to make them worse. But he understood. For suddenly, with that immemorial gesture of his, he handed us a pot of his honey to squeeze in on top of the rest—and somehow that moved us as much as anything.

"Is it all right about the boots?" I asked Sam. His face clouded. This was a moment he had been dreading. For the only time probably in his life he had not been as good as his word. Silently, miserably, he unwrapped a bundle and laid one pair of old boots on the cave floor. The man, he muttered, had *promised* two pairs . . . He couldn't look us in the face. He would try someone else tomorrow, if we liked to wait. But boots, these days, were as scarce as pigs . . .

Mark and I stood staring at the pair. We stared at one another. I wanted those boots so much, I couldn't bring myself to say a word. Then Mark picked them up and laughed. "I gate-crashed the party," he said. "Anyone else but you two would have bumped me off months ago. After all," he said, "the whole of civilization depends on *someone* being prepared to give way." And he handed the boots to me.

CHAPTER XVI

"Oh, hallo, I didn't expect you back so soon." Matthew was in the hotel lounge, gloomily watching a football match being played in Rome by floodlight and, apparently, in a snowstorm.

"Get your call through to Florence O.K.?"

"Yes, thanks. What a bloody invention the television is. Worse even than the wireless and the internal combustion engine. How were the peasants?"

"Oh, they were fine. Let's go and eat."

"And your friend Sam?" he asked when we were into a greasy *pastina in brodo*.

"Quite unchanged, really. In essentials. A little older, with a pot belly and a crooked arm—from being run over. A typical American of about sixty—except that he still speaks English in the same inimitable way. We didn't recognize one another at first. I've altered a lot more than he has, of course, with my white hair. He never had much hair."

"Why must we have a radio in the dining-room as well as the television going full blast outside? See your hayloft?"

"Prestige. The guests expect it. No, the old house is derelict. The roof fallen in—a ruin. It became impossible for his wife on her own. Antonio built her a little concrete bungalow on the other side of the road from his house. Mark warned me about that. Sam and Antonio hid him for a further six months after Amos and I left. He's kept in touch with them better than I have. He was here a couple of years ago, that was before Sam got back, and he wrote me afterwards. He had a meal with Antonio, who asked why he'd come to the Abruzzi. Mark told him the truth. 'But I've come simply to see *you*.' Antonio stared at him, unbelievingly. Then two tears rolled down his cheek. Mark was much moved. Incidentally, he said he climbed to the cave—rather a good effort."

"On his own?"

"Presumably. He didn't mention anyone else."

We wrestled with a mess of veal in tomatoes and drank a bottle of one of those factory-produced wines described on some labels, as "*adulterato*," on others as "*sophisticato*," the terms being, it seems, synonymous in the wine industry.

"But Sam is happy?" asked Matthew.

"Very, so far as I could judge. Nice little bungalow, half an acre of land, and a wire netting fence with concrete posts to keep trespassers out. The house is far better for his wife—she has terrible asthma. A charming gentle person, very shy. She was never really tough enough for their existence before. They have a fridge, an electric cooker and radiator—every mod. con. Sam was delighted with the gadgets. They'll have the telly soon. He's already knocked the garden into shape—I saw his runner beans, lettuces, marrows. He's given up farming—can afford not to, I gathered."

"I see. And Antonio?"

"Much the same, I thought. His wife too. He still farms a bit—hires out tractors and a threshing machine. But he's chiefly building—it's more profitable. He's a versatile chap and wonderfully active for seventy. We drove to look at some of his breeze-block bungalows. Tiled bathrooms are what he's proudest of. We flushed a dozen loos. Two daughters are married in Venezuela. I saw the photos. I wouldn't have recognized them of course, nor the husband of one whom I knew as a youth called Dionino. All very prosperous. Antonio's son Manfredo is just back from there on a visit. Rather browned off, I'm afraid, when his father detailed him to take us up the mountain, but he can show off his English."

"And did you feel their pattern of life had changed for the better?"

"Certainly. I don't expect them to continue feeding escaped prisoners for ever. They both asked me to dinner but I tactfully explained

I couldn't. Probably they were relieved. The situation is a little tricky. They live twenty yards apart and aren't on speaking terms."

"But I thought they were such friends."

"Were. When Sam got back he thought Antonio had diddled him out of a bit of land in his absence. 'That's not *right*,' he said to me. He's suing him. I tried to keep out of it. I saw first one, then the other, gave them news of my children, asked after theirs—and pushed off."

"So you're depressed?"

"Not in the least. I adore them both—though I'm sad they've quarreled. Let's finish this ghastly meal and go for the dodgems."

The fair was in full swing, the blaze of winking colored lights obscuring Morrone and transforming the houses round the Piazza Garibaldi into pale grey and yellow cliffs. The aqueduct might have been a Covent Garden stage set, the ruined stump of San Francesco della Scarpa a backdrop painted against a thunderous night sky. There were shooting booths where accuracy with an airgun gained you a ringed dove or even a golden pheasant; dodgems; the Whip; a Giant Wheel; whatever those centrifugal aeroplanes are called; and of course mechanical claws where, if you pressed the lever at the right moment, you were presented with a diamond necklace or a wrist-watch. Has *anyone* ever won? Perhaps the most amusing side-show were miniature racing cars on a figure of eight switchback. After being pulled uphill electrically, you drove recklessly down. Matthew could not have enough of his arch-enemy the motor-car in this form. Since he tried to steer his like a camel he created chaos and a gang of attendants had to rescue him off the track every time to avoid serious accidents. A dozen loudspeakers blared popular tunes of the moment, the crowd shouted, jostled, and laughed in a fashion that, for some reason, is more fun in Italy than in England. We enjoyed ourselves no end.

We drifted to a booth where a group of young men, with much self-conscious male pride, demonstrated the strength of their fists on a punch-ball. "I suppose I'm too old," sighed Matthew, itching to demonstrate the strength of his fist, but hesitating in case he couldn't excel mere *giovanotti*. While he stood struggling with his male pride, I watched the merry-go-round, a splendid rotating palace complete with decorated organ and three rows of stampeding white horses. The sophisticated young fought shy of anything so juvenile, at any rate the riders seemed to be mostly older peasants, the men in caps, the women wearing scarves or shawls. A shining bald head flashed past, bobbing up and down. It belonged to a small round elderly man in a neat dark suit, his arm encircling the waist of a pretty girl on the next steed. He, at least, looked exactly the same after twenty years.

The music and the horses were slowing down. "I must leave you for ten minutes," I said to Matthew. "I've just seen an old acquaintance, the headmaster of the largest school here. I tried to contact him this morning but the school was closed because of the *festa*. I'd intended to try tomorrow afternoon but I know we'll be in a rush by then. Now's the perfect chance—it avoids the question of hospitality and I don't want to get too heavily involved."

"You'll find me on the racing cars again. I'll be happy there for as long as you like."

Il professore was puffing from the equestrian exercise and obviously couldn't place me at first though he flashed a friendly smile. The girl hovered in the background. She could have been his daughter but probably was not, as he didn't attempt to introduce her. Doubtless a pupil. "Back in a minute," he said to her in Italian and to me, in English, "Let me see, when did we last . . ."

"In Intradacqua. Before that in Vasco."

An old memory stirred. "Ah, yes. Of course. So we meet in Sulmona at last!" He was still having to guess hard to keep pace. "Didn't you know *Tenente* Duffy? He was out here with a friend the year before last."

"Certainly. He gave me your present address . . ." And we chatted pleasantly for a few minutes about Mark's recent visit, about the good old days in the prison camp. His wife and children still lived in Vasco. He was only in Sulmona during term time. "I always love a merry-go-round, don't you?" he said, politely talking to cover up the blank in his memory of me. "I find it—a symbol of our whole existence. It provides an illusion of freedom but with a reassurance, also, of security. The horses are as exciting to ride as live horses, but more controllable. You think you're moving forward, when all the time you're going round and round."

The girl continued to hover and it was unfair to detain him. "I suppose, when you were hiding here at the end of 1943, you never came across someone called Frank Del Signore?"

No, he couldn't recall meeting anyone of that name. Of course, there was the famous film director in Rome—presumably I wasn't thinking of him?

"Is there a film director called Del Signore?" I asked.

But one of the best. Surely I'd seen—and he quoted a string of Italian film titles.

"Alas, I'm ashamed to say I haven't. But I shall bear them in mind," I said. "There's one other person you might be able to give me news of—Lieutenant Croce. The interpreter at Vasco."

He chuckled, not very kindly. Oh, old Croce. Of course he remembered him.

"He's not, by any chance, a captain in the *carabiniere*?"

Good heavens, no. Croce was still in hospital when Rome fell. His house in Pescara was bombed, his estate near L'Aquila confiscated. Fancy my remembering Croce. He'd left the Abruzzi at the end of the war. The last *il professore* had heard of him he was out in Sicily, more or less destitute, working for a circus or something of that kind. A sad story. But, after all, he'd been a Fascist . . . Now, what were my plans? Could he offer me dinner tomorrow?

"Alas, I'm just passing through. But next time."

"*Next* time, then," he said eagerly. "Without fail." We shook hands and I returned to watch Matthew, seated in his car, being pulled off the center of the race track by the breakdown gang.

"What about bed?" I said.

"Let's just try the Theater of the Quadrumans. The curtain's up now—I saw people going in. I think it's a marionette show—or perhaps a contortionist."

To our disappointment, the theater proved to be simply a few performing monkeys. The atmosphere inside the booth was stifling, the throng of spectators so dense that we got no nearer than the door. I saw nothing whatever. Matthew, who can't bear any wild animal, even a monkey, doing tricks, peered over the heads of the crowd for a few moments, then abruptly left.

"Just four chimps dressed up in clothes and playing the fool," he said when we were outside. "But their keeper was the first person I've seen in the Abruzzi with a striking face. Thin tall chap with a lit-

tle pointed beard and an extraordinarily arrogant manner. He positively sneered, as if he loathed the whole thing but us most of all. I
suppose the poor devil has to do it for a living. He'd lost an arm."

"The left or right?"

"The right, I think. Yes, I'm sure. Why?"

"Oh, nothing. I just wondered. One of my ghosts. But I'll let
that one lie. Well, shall we get back? I said we'd pick up Manfredo
at eight sharp."

Manfredo looked more browned off than ever by the time, half an
hour late, he'd been fetched out of bed. Antonio, also sleepy-eyed,
stood outside the house in his pyjamas to watch us set off. There was
no sign of Sam in his bungalow behind its wire and concrete fence.
I suspected he was deliberately keeping out of sight in the garden at
the back. We parked the car farther down the road, in the shelter of
a bungalow Antonio was building, walked up past Sam's old house,
then along the old familiar track.

We'd started too late, the sun was already high, and I soon
began to find the pack with our lunch too heavy for comfort. It
wasn't much of a load, about half what I'd carried the last time with
Amos, but Manfredo had calmly added a large flask of wine which
weighed more than the rest together. When Matthew had offered
to carry it I'd insisted. This was *my* expedition. Manfredo clearly
did not intend to help. It was enough that he should be expected to
spend most of the day guiding us up the very mountain that, probably, he had migrated to Venezuela to escape from. His pointed croc-
odile-skin shoes, well-creased gaberdine trousers, and snazzy sports
jacket eloquently expressed his utter disapproval of the whole bloody
silly idea.

"We must just call in at Adullam," I said. He doubted if he could
find it—hadn't been there for years, since boyhood. We wasted more
time and effort searching for it in the rough scrub. I'd forgotten how
difficult it was to reach. We overshot it, had to scramble a hundred
feet down a cliff face to get there. It looked much as before, and
probably had not been used since our day. The charcoal drawings
were still visible, if you peered hard enough. Near the entrance a
large black snake—perhaps the same snake—lay curled on the same
rock. Manfredo angrily threw a stone and it streaked out of sight.

The hill upwards from Adullam was steeper than I remembered—but then I'd been younger then . . . Every so often I rested for a second or two, to consider the pattern of fields below, needing to assure myself that they were indeed beautiful. But then I'd given up abstract painting years back. The bare face of Rotella across the valley, scarred with its viaducts, was beautiful also—but I couldn't help thinking I preferred the rolling hopfields between Farnham, Surrey, and Alton, Hants. Matthew forged on ahead with the leisurely stride of someone used to covering his thirty miles a day. Manfredo followed him, in sullen silence, but determined not to lag behind on his native mountain. Let them try carrying this pack, I growled to myself. The scrub was hot and airless, the loose stones on the track continually slipped underfoot, and each stumble jarred my whole body. At one point I decided I couldn't lift my legs one yard farther. My eyes were popping from my head and if I didn't give in I'd rupture a blood vessel. Five minutes farther I decided I didn't care if I did rupture a blood vessel. If I could only reach the halfway mark, the fig tree where we'd stopped with Gabriele that first time, honor would be satisfied.

Suddenly the air had become cooler, the scrub less stifling. Not so far ahead, after all, I could see Matthew and Manfredo seated among the wild lavender. The ridge and furrow marks still showed through the stones and dried grass, but the fig tree no longer bore fruit. It was dead. Only one or two withered last-year's leaves trembled in the strong breeze. "It's old. It's finished," said Manfredo. The comment struck me as uncalled-for. "Well, come on, my turn to carry the pack," said Matthew. And I handed it over without protest.

It was worth carrying the pack for the pleasure of not carrying it. For the rest of the way my body felt feather-light, borne over the mountain's shoulder by the wind. The gorge from Pettorano appeared to our left. Then a last long scramble over the shale, clinging to dwarf beeches to help ourselves across, and we were there. Four and a half hours. But we'd wasted at least half an hour finding Adullam. We flopped down on the ledge of turf at the cave mouth and I glanced at Matthew, to see how he was looking. Not, of course, as exhausted as Manfredo and myself. But I think he was glad we'd arrived; certainly glad of lunch.

"You say Sam and Antonio came up here with food for you about twice a week?" asked Matthew when we were refreshed. "For *six weeks?*"

"Yes. The latter half under snow."

"Well, I'll take your word for it. But all I can say is I'm damned if I would have done—even for my mother and Luke."

The shelter had long since vanished. The cave, enlarged by Yellow Peril, was still too small for comfort, as I crawled in a moment to examine some initials scratched on the smoke-blackened surface. Twenty years' worth of leaves had blown on to the floor and rotted. It was all as impersonal to me now as the photo of some house by the sea where one once spent a holiday in childhood. We could see a shepherd and his sheep camped in the beech clump in the little valley below. I pointed out the route up to the *fontana*, the entrance to the gorge to Pettorano. "Let's take that way down. It's so much quicker," said Manfredo. "There's a house at the bottom which sells American canned beer."

With the food and wine Manfredo unbent, grew talkative. He was going back to Venezuela if his father could spare him. He was obviously a devoted son. But, he said, you couldn't earn enough money in the Abruzzi. Were things so bad? Not so bad as they had been a few years ago. But still . . . There was no opportunity. No life, really . . . He was a virile handsome young man of twenty-eight, the image of Antonio at the same age, I imagined. I pointed to the dust on his shoes, the scratches on his trousers, and said I was sorry. Oh, that's nothing . . . He remembered the war clearly, his climbs to this cave and others. Now that had been an exciting time! I mentioned the quarrel between Sam and his father. He laughed, tolerantly. Oh, well. These foolish old men. Both were a bit at fault. Perhaps at heart they rather enjoyed it even. But Baldo, he'd often been told, was never quite the same after his eldest son died. He hadn't known Florindo well but he remembered him clearly and people still talked of him. "*Everyone* loved Lindo. He was *everyone's* friend." He shrugged his broad shoulders. To lose a son must be a great loss for a man, he said.

It was, I said.

We had a few minutes before we needed to start back. I wanted to allow time to say goodbye to Antonio and Sam and take their photographs. While Manfredo lay down for a quick snooze, Matthew and I crouched in the cave mouth, for the wind was cold.

"Well, it's a good spot," he said. "I'm so glad you brought me. It must be an odd feeling to be here. I can understand why you were so keen to visit it again."

"I wouldn't have got here without you. At one point farther down I reckoned I'd had it. I only kept going from the sort of obstinacy one has about letting a friend get the better of one. I was thinking of Mark too. He's a couple of years older than me and did it two years ago. I don't suppose he walks a mile in a month. If he could do it, I could.

"But there was a better reason, really, than that," I said, or perhaps I didn't say, it comes to the same. "A better reason than sentiment also—than just revisiting a place that has meant much to my life. I wanted so much to reach this cave, once more, for something else. You would call it superstitious nonsense—and you'd probably be right. I can only explain it this way. Twenty years ago, as I told you yesterday, I made a sort of pact with Providence. I asked for the peace to last twenty years. And I have *willed* for it to last with every ounce of my being. I've had my turn—and a good turn. I ask nothing more for myself. But I want twenty more years for my children, for Sam's and Antonio's children, for everyone's children. I am a pretty useless member of society, a creative pessimist, a sort of bluebottle buzzing round the head of a carthorse that's pulling a heavy load uphill. Being more intelligent, presumably, than a bluebottle, I don't delude myself, any more than I delude the horse, that my contribution is of the slightest help. Still, I have to *pretend* to believe that it is. It sounds silly, I know—like a child hoping to stave off disaster by always stepping on the joins in a pavement—but, for me, to climb to this cave had that kind of significance. And, by the skin of my teeth, I've got here. I wonder if Mark came up for a similarly absurd reason? One day, if we ever meet again, I must ask him . . ."

But Matthew was not listening. He had leant back to examine something scratched on the blackened surface—and I was rather sorry, for I didn't wish to spoil his little surprise.

"There have been trippers up here since your day," he said. "They've scraped the initials M.D. and H.K. October 1961."

"Mark Duffy—to prove he'd made it. I can't think of anyone with the initials H. K. Except of course Henry Kempster."

"Here, let's finish the *vino*." Matthew was trying to hide a grin. "I hadn't meant to tell you this till we got back to Florence. On that train—Henry *wasn't* shot. He gave his scarf to another Yugoslav—who was in fact the German stooge who had betrayed him. Mark had the idea—and it must have needed nerve to carry out. But Henry knew it was his only chance. He stayed on the train till somewhere near Florence—Bologna, I believe. Zozo hid him in the cellars for six months. You see, I'd no idea you didn't know the story. I've heard it so often myself!"

Matthew watched for my astonishment. But I was too tired to oblige.

"I'm sorry," I said. "But I guessed yesterday. Your face when I mentioned Henry Kempster. I can always tell when you see a chance of pulling my leg. I remembered something else. The corpse under the sack was wearing hobnailed boots. Kempster had rubber-soled parachuting boots . . . And then the schoolmaster at the fair last night confirmed it. But in a way I think I always knew he had survived. Where is he these days?"

"Married, with a large family. He lives in Florence. You'll see him at my wedding."

Now Matthew had succeeded in surprising me.

"At *your* wedding?"

"Yes. Didn't I tell you? I'm marrying Zozo tomorrow afternoon."

CPSIA information can be obtained
at www.ICGtesting.com
Printed in the USA
LVHW010957301118
598771LV00001B/1/P

9 781589 881327